Rec

**Ten stories on five themes
Edited by
Alex Adkins and Mark Shackleton**

Edward Arnold
A division of Hodder & Stoughton
LONDON   BALTIMORE   MELBOURNE   AUCKLAND

© 1980 Alex Adkins and Mark Shackleton

First published in Great Britain 1980
Reprinted 1981, 1983, 1984, 1986, 1987, 1988

British Library Cataloguing Publication Data

Recollections
 1. English language – Text-books for foreigners
 2. Readers
 I. Adkins, Alex   II. Shackleton, Mark
 428′.6′4   PE1128

 ISBN 0-7131-8021-8

All rights reserved. No part of this publication may be reproduced
or transmitted in any form or by any means, electronically or
mechanically, including photocopying, recording or any
information storage or retrieval system, without either prior
permission in writing from the publisher or a licence permitting
restricted copying. In the United Kingdom such licences are
issued by the Copyright Licensing Agency: 33–34 Alfred Place,
London WC1E 7DP.

Typeset in 10/11pt Journal Roman. Printed and bound in Great
Britain for Edward Arnold, the educational, academic and medical
publishing division of Hodder and Stoughton Limited, 41 Bedford
Square, London WC1B 3DQ by Richard Clay Ltd, Bungay,
Suffolk.

Introduction

Recollections is a collection of short stories covering five themes. While the ten stories were chosen for their intrinsic merit, care has also been taken to ensure that the level of English throughout is one accessible to the higher intermediate reader of English as a foreign or second language. They are also suitable for the native English speaker who may wish to read for study or pleasure. Not all the stories are of equal linguistic difficulty. Those by Joyce and Mansfield are probably the most demanding.

Each theme is explored in two stories. This allows the reader to consider the treatment of an idea from two different viewpoints — for example, Roald Dahl approaches the theme of conflict with characteristic black humour, whilst John Steinbeck tackles the same theme with tough realism.

Question material on each story is intended to assist (and not to test) comprehension and appreciation. For this reason, a more demanding main question is usually followed by a series of easier questions which, step by step, help the reader build up an understanding of the issues raised by the main question. The easier questions are primarily for the reader working alone; the main questions are possible starting points for group discussion. The glossaries give explanations *in context* and are intended to help the reader read fluently and with enjoyment.

It is, of course, appropriate and desirable that students should feel free, after considering the stories themselves, to move to a discussion of topics suggested by the stories but in relation to their own opinions and experience. These general questions (as, perhaps, a discussion of the problems of adolescence arising out of 'Through the Tunnel') are not given here as it is felt that their imposition on a class, regardless of the circumstances of those involved, is not the best way of generating interest. It is initially up to the teacher, who knows the people concerned, to provide opportunities for them to explore such issues as appropriate.

Explanations of some terms used in the glossaries

abbr.: abbreviation. Shortening of a word or phrase.

A.E.: American English.

archaic: old and no longer in normal use.

coll.: colloquial. Used to describe the kind of language appropriate to informal speech.

idiom.: idiomatic. An idiom is a phrase, usually found in colloquial speech, whose meaning cannot be worked out by knowledge of the meanings of the individual words. E.g., 'to be browned off' means 'to feel irritated and impatient'.

ironic: having a deeper meaning different from the normal understanding of what is said.

metaphor: a colourful use of language in which something is described in terms of something else. E.g., 'It was a beautiful day; *the sun smiled down* on the holiday-makers'.

* * * * *

Where there are phonetic transcriptions for words in the glossaries, the International Phonetic Alphabet has been used.

Innocence and Experience

Doris Lessing (1919—)

Doris Lessing is a British writer, born in Persia. In 1924 her family moved to Rhodesia to farm there. She began to write while living in Rhodesia but did not become a professional author until after moving to Britain in 1949. Many of her novels and stories are based on her experience of Southern Africa and its racial problems. One of the best known is 'The Grass is Singing' (1950). She is also interested in exploring relationships between men and women and the life of independent women in contemporary western society. Her novels also include 'The Golden Notebook' (1962), the 'Children of Violence' series (1952—69), 'Briefing for a Descent into Hell' (1971) and 'The Summer Before the Dark' (1973). She has written a number of short stories which appear in the following collections: 'Five' (1953), 'African Stories' (1964), 'The Story of a Non-Marrying Man' (1972) and 'The Habit of Loving' (1957), from which 'Through the Tunnel' is taken.

The story

Jerry is on holiday abroad with his widowed mother. He meets a group of local youths, older than himself. He becomes obsessed with the need to be more like them and his desire takes the form of a trial of endurance — swimming through an underwater tunnel. The tunnel is long and dangerous; if he fails he will certainly drown.

Through the Tunnel

Going to the shore on the first morning of the holiday, the young English boy stopped at a turning of the path and looked down at a wild and rocky bay,* and then over to the crowded beach he knew so well from other years. His mother walked on in front of him, carrying a bright-striped bag in one hand. Her other arm, swinging loose, was very white in the sun. The boy watched that white, naked arm, and turned his eyes, which had a frown behind them, toward the bay and back again to his mother. When she felt he was not with her, she swung around. 'Oh, there you are, Jerry!' she said. She looked impatient, then smiled. 'Why, darling, would you rather not come with me? Would you rather—' She frowned, conscientiously worrying over what amusements he might secretly be longing for which she had been too busy or too careless to imagine. He was very familiar with that anxious, apologetic smile. Contrition* sent him running after her. And yet, as he ran, he looked back over his shoulder at the wild bay; and all morning, as he played on the safe beach, he was thinking of it.

Next morning, when it was time for the routine of swimming and sunbathing, his mother said, 'Are you tired of the usual beach, Jerry? Would you like to go somewhere else?'

'Oh, no!' he said quickly, smiling at her out of that unfailing impulse of contrition* — a sort of chivalry. Yet, walking down the path with her, he blurted out, 'I'd like to go and have a look at those rocks down there.'

She gave the idea her attention. It was a wild-looking place, and there was no one there, but she said, 'Of course, Jerry. When you've had enough, come to the big beach. Or just go straight back to the villa, if you like.' She walked away, that bare arm, now slightly reddened from yesterday's sun, swinging. And he almost ran after her again, feeling it unbearable that she should go by herself, but he did not.

She was thinking, Of course he's old enough to be safe without me. Have I been keeping him too close? He mustn't feel he ought to be with me. I must be careful.

4 *Innocence and Experience*

He was an only child, eleven years old. She was a widow. She was determined to be neither possessive nor lacking in devotion.* She went worrying off to her beach.

As for Jerry, once he saw that his mother had gained her beach, he began the steep descent to the bay. From where he was, high up among red-brown rocks, it was a scoop of moving bluish green fringed with white. As he went lower, he saw that it spread among small promontories and inlets* of rough, sharp rock, and the crisping, lapping surface showed stains of purple and darker blue. Finally, as he ran sliding and scraping down the last few yards, he saw an edge of white surf, and the shallow, luminous movement of water over white sand, and, beyond that, a solid, heavy blue.

He ran straight into the water and began swimming. He was a good swimmer. He went out fast over the gleaming sand, over a middle region where rocks lay like discoloured monsters under the surface, and then he was in the real sea — a warm sea where irregular cold currents from the deep water shocked his limbs.

When he was so far out that he could look back not only on the little bay but past the promontory that was between it and the big beach, he floated on the buoyant surface and looked for his mother. There she was, a speck of yellow under an umbrella that looked like a slice of orange peel. He swam back to shore, relieved at being sure she was there, but all at once very lonely.

On the edge of a small cape* that marked the side of the bay away from the promontory was a loose scatter of rocks. Above them, some boys were stripping off their clothes. They came running, naked, down to the rocks. The English boy swam towards them, and kept his distance at a stone's throw.* They were of that coast, all of them burned smooth dark brown, and speaking a language he did not understand. To be with them, of them, was a craving* that filled his whole body. He swam a little closer; they turned and watched him with narrowed, alert dark eyes. Then one smiled and waved. It was enough. In a minute, he had swum in and was on the rocks beside them, smiling with a desperate, nervous supplication.* They shouted cheerful greetings at him, and then, as he preserved his nervous, uncomprehending smile, they understood that he was a foreigner strayed from his own beach, and they proceeded to forget him. But he was happy. He was with them.

They began diving again and again from a high point into a well of blue sea between rough, pointed rocks. After they had dived and come up, they swam around, hauled themselves up, and waited their turn to dive again. They were big boys — men to Jerry. He dived, and they watched him, and when he swam around to take his place, they made way for him. He felt he was accepted, and he dived again, carefully, proud of himself.

Soon the biggest of the boys poised* himself, shot down into the water, and did not come up. The others stood about, watching. Jerry, after waiting for the sleek brown head to appear, let out a yell of warning; they looked at him idly and turned their eyes back towards the water. After a long time, the boy came up on the other side of a big dark rock, letting the air out of his lungs in a spluttering gasp and a shout of triumph. Immediately, the rest of them dived in. One moment, the morning seemed full of chattering boys; the next, the air and the surface of the water were empty. But through the heavy blue, dark shapes could be seen moving and groping.*

Jerry dived, shot past the school* of underwater swimmers, saw a black wall of rock looming at him, touched it, and bobbed up at once to the surface, where the wall was a low barrier he could see across. There was no one visible; under him, in the water, the dim shapes of the swimmers had disappeared. Then one, and then another of the boys came up on the far side of the barrier of rock, and he understood that they had swum through some gap or hole in it. He plunged down again. He could see nothing through the stinging* salt water but the blank rock. When he came up, the boys were all on the diving rock, preparing to attempt the feat* again. And now, in a panic of failure, he yelled up, in English, 'Look at me! Look!' and he began splashing and kicking in the water like a foolish dog.

They looked down gravely, frowning. He knew the frown. At moments of failure, when he clowned to claim his mother's attention, it was with just this grave, embarrassed inspection that she rewarded him. Through his hot shame, feeling the pleading grin on his face like a scar that he could never remove, he looked up at the group of big brown boys on the rock and shouted, *'Bonjour! Merci! Au revoir! Monsieur, monsieur!'** while he hooked his fingers round his ears and waggled* them.

Water surged into his mouth; he choked, sank, came up. The rock, lately weighed with boys, seemed to rear up out of the water as their weight was removed. They were flying down past him, now, into the water; the air was full of falling bodies. Then the rock was empty in the hot sunlight. He counted one, two, three. . . .

At fifty, he was terrified. They must all be drowning beneath him, in the watery caves of the rock! At a hundred, he stared around him at the empty hillside, wondering if he should yell for help. He counted faster, faster, to hurry them up, to bring them to the surface quickly, to drown them quickly — anything rather than the terror of counting on and on into the blue emptiness of the morning. And then, at a hundred and sixty, the water beyond the rock was full of boys blowing like brown whales. They swam back to the shore without a look at him.

He climbed back to the diving rock and sat down, feeling the hot roughness of it under his thighs.* The boys were gathering up their bits of clothing and running off along the shore to another promontory. They were leaving to get away from him. He cried openly, fists in his eyes. There was no one to see him, and he cried himself out.

It seemed to him that a long time had passed, and he swam out to where he could see his mother. Yes, she was still there, a yellow spot under an orange umbrella. He swam back to the big rock, climbed up, and dived into the blue pool among the fanged* and angry boulders. Down he went, until he touched the wall of rock again. But the salt was so painful in his eyes that he could not see.

He came to the surface, swam to shore and went back to the villa to wait for his mother. Soon she walked slowly up the path, swinging her striped bag, the flushed,* naked arm dangling beside her. 'I want some swimming goggles,' he panted, defiant and beseeching.*

She gave him a patient, inquisitive look as she said casually, 'Well, of course, darling.'

But now, now, now! He must have them this minute, and no other time. He nagged and pestered* until she went with him to a shop. As soon as she had bought the goggles, he grabbed them from her hand as if she were going to claim them for herself, and was off, running down the steep path to the bay.

Jerry swam out to the big barrier rock, adjusted the goggles, and dived. The impact of the water broke the rubber-enclosed vacuum, and the goggles came loose. He understood that he must swim down to the base of the rock from the surface of the water. He fixed the goggles tight and firm, filled his lungs, and floated, face down, on the water. Now he could see. It was as if he had eyes of a different kind — fish-eyes that showed everything clear and delicate and wavering in the bright water.

Under him, six or seven feet down, was a floor of perfectly clean, shining white sand, rippled firm and hard by the tides. Two greyish shapes steered there, like long, rounded pieces of wood or slate. They were fish. He saw them nose towards each other, poise motionless, make a dart forward, swerve off, and come around again. It was like a water dance. A few inches above them, the water sparkled as if sequins* were dropping through it. Fish again — myriads of minute* fish, the length of his fingernail, were drifting through the water, and in a moment he could feel the innumerable tiny touches of them against his limbs. It was like swimming in flaked silver. The great rock the big boys had swum through rose sheer* out of the white sand, black, tufted lightly with greenish weed. He could see no gap in it. He swam down to its base.

Again and again he rose, took a big chestful of air, and went down. Again and again he groped over the surface of the rock, feeling it, almost hugging it* in the desperate need to find the entrance. And then, once, while he was clinging to the black wall, his knees came up and he shot his feet out forward and they met no obstacle.* He had found the hole.

He gained the surface, clambered about the stones that littered the barrier rock until he found a big one, and, with this in his arms, let himself down over the side of the rock. He dropped, with the weight, straight to the sandy floor. Clinging tight to the anchor of stone, he lay on his side and looked in under the dark shelf at the place where his feet had gone. He could see the hole. It was an irregular, dark gap, but he could not see deep into it. He let go of his anchor,* clung with his hands to the edges of the hole, and tried to push himself in.

He got his head in, found his shoulders jammed,* moved them in sidewise, and was inside as far as his waist. He could see nothing ahead. Something soft and clammy* touched his mouth, he saw a dark frond* moving against the greyish rock, and panic filled him. He thought of octopuses, of clinging weed. He pushed himself out backward and caught a glimpse, as he retreated, of a harmless tentacle of seaweed drifting in the mouth of the tunnel. But it was enough. He reached the sunlight, swam to shore, and lay on the diving rock. He looked down into the blue well of water. He knew he must find his way through that cave, or hole, or tunnel, and out the other side.

First, he thought, he must learn to control his breathing. He let himself down into the water with another big stone in his arms, so that he could lie effortlessly on the bottom of the sea. He counted. One, two, three. He counted steadily. He could hear the movement of blood in his chest. Fifty-one, fifty-two. . . . His chest was hurting. He let go of the rock and went up into the air. He saw that the sun was low. He rushed to the villa and found his mother at her supper. She said only 'Did you enjoy yourself?' and he said 'Yes.'

All night, the boy dreamed of the water-filled cave in the rock, and as soon as breakfast was over he went to the bay.

That night, his nose bled badly. For hours he had been underwater, learning to hold his breath, and now he felt weak and dizzy.* His mother said, 'I shouldn't overdo things, darling, if I were you.'

That day and the next, Jerry exercised his lungs as if everything, the whole of his life, all that he would become, depended upon it. And again his nose bled at night, and his mother insisted on his coming with her the next day. It was a torment* to him to waste a day of his careful self-training, but he stayed with her on that other beach, which now seemed a place for small children, a place where his mother might lie safe in the sun. It was not his beach.

He did not ask for permission, on the following day, to go to his beach. He went, before his mother could consider the complicated rights and wrongs of the matter. A day's rest, he discovered, had improved his count by ten. The big boys had made the passage while he counted a hundred and sixty. He had been counting fast, in his fright. Probably now, if he tried, he could get through that long tunnel, but he was not going to try yet. A curious, most unchildlike persistence, a controlled impatience, made him wait. In the meantime, he lay underwater on the white sand, littered now by stones he had brought down from the upper air, and studied the entrance to the tunnel. He knew every jut and corner of it, as far as it was possible to see. It was as if he already felt its sharpness about his shoulders.

He sat by the clock in the villa, when his mother was not near, and checked his time. He was incredulous* and then proud to find he could hold his breath without strain for two minutes. The words 'two minutes', authorized by the clock, brought the adventure that was so necessary to him close.

In another four days, his mother said casually one morning, they must go home. On the day before they left, he would do it. He would do it if it killed him, he said defiantly to himself. But two days before they were to leave — a day of triumph when he increased his count by fifteen — his nose bled so badly that he turned dizzy and had to lie limply over the big rock like a bit of seaweed, watching the thick red blood flow on to the rock and trickle slowly down to the sea. He was frightened. Supposing he turned dizzy in the tunnel? Supposing he died there, trapped? Supposing — his head went around, in the hot sun, and he almost gave up. He thought he would return to the house and lie down, and next summer, perhaps, when he had another year's growth in him — *then* he would go through the hole.

But even after he had made the decision, or thought he had, he found himself sitting up on the rock and looking down into the water, and he knew that now, this moment when his nose had only just stopped bleeding, when his head was still sore and throbbing* — this was the moment when he would try. If he did not do it now, he never would. He was trembling with fear that he would not go, and he was trembling with horror at that long,

long tunnel under the rock, under the sea. Even in the open sunlight, the barrier rock seemed very wide and very heavy; tons of rock pressed down on where he would go. If he died there, he would lie until one day — perhaps not before next year — those big boys would swim into it and find it blocked.

He put on his goggles, fitted them tight, tested the vacuum. His hands were shaking. Then he chose the biggest stone he could carry and slipped over the edge of the rock until half of him was in the cool, enclosing water and half in the hot sun. He looked up once at the empty sky, filled his lungs once, twice, and then sank fast to the bottom with the stone. He let it go and began to count. He took the edges of the hole in his hands and drew himself into it, wriggling* his shoulders in sidewise as he remembered he must, kicking himself along with his feet.

Soon he was clear inside. He was in a small rock-bound* hole filled with yellowish-grey water. The water was pushing him up against the roof. The roof was sharp and pained his back. He pulled himself along with his hands — fast, fast — and used his legs as levers. His head knocked against something; a sharp pain dizzied him. Fifty, fifty-one, fifty-two. . . . He was without light, and the water seemed to press upon him with the weight of rock. Seventy-one, seventy-two. . . . There was no strain on his lungs.* He felt like an inflated balloon, his lungs were so light and easy, but his head was pulsing.*

He was being continually pressed against the sharp roof, which felt slimy* as well as sharp. Again he thought of octopuses, and wondered if the tunnel might be filled with weed that could tangle* him. He gave himself a panicky,* convulsive kick forward, ducked his head, and swam. His feet and hands moved freely, as if in open water. The hole must have widened out. He thought he must be swimming fast, and he was frightened of banging his head if the tunnel narrowed.

A hundred, a hundred and one. . . The water paled.* Victory filled him. His lungs were beginning to hurt. A few more strokes and he would be out. He was counting wildly; he said a hundred and fifteen, and then, a long time later, a hundred and fifteen again. The water was a clear jewel-green all around him. Then he saw, above his head, a crack running up through the rock. Sunlight was falling through it, showing the clean dark rock of the tunnel, a single mussel shell, and darkness ahead.

He was at the end of what he could do. He looked up at the crack as if it were filled with air and not water, as if he could put his mouth to it to draw in air. A hundred and fifteen, he heard himself say inside his head — but he had said that long ago. He must go on into the blackness ahead, or he would drown. His head was swelling, his lungs cracking. A hundred and fifteen, a hundred and fifteen pounded* through his head, and he feebly* clutched at rocks in the dark, pulling himself forward, leaving the brief space of sunlit water behind. He felt he was dying. He was no longer quite conscious. He struggled on in the darkness between lapses into unconsciousness. An immense, swelling* pain filled his head, and then the darkness cracked with an explosion of green light. His hands, groping forward, met nothing, and his feet, kicking back, propelled him out into the open sea.

He drifted to the surface, his face turned up to the air. He was gasping like a fish. He felt he would sink now and drown; he could not swim the few feet back to the rock. Then he was clutching it and pulling himself up on it. He lay face down, gasping. He could see nothing but a red-veined, clotted dark. His eyes must have burst, he thought; they were full of blood. He tore off his goggles and a gout of blood went into the sea. His nose was bleeding, and the blood had filled the goggles.

He scooped up handfuls of water from the cool, salty sea, to splash on his face, and did not know whether it was blood or salt water he tasted. After a time, his heart quieted, his eyes cleared, and he sat up. He could see the local boys diving and playing half a mile away. He did not want them. He wanted nothing but to get back home and lie down.

In a short while, Jerry swam to shore and climbed slowly up the path to the villa. He flung* himself on his bed and slept, waking at the sound of feet on the path outside. His mother was coming back. He rushed to the bathroom, thinking she must not see his face with bloodstains, or tearstains, on it. He came out of the bathroom and met her as she walked into the villa, smiling, her eyes lighting up.

'Have a nice morning?' she asked, laying her head on his warm brown shoulder a moment.

'Oh, yes, thank you,' he said.

'You look a bit pale.' And then, sharp and anxious. 'How did you bang your head?'

'Oh, just banged it,' he told her.

She looked at him closely. He was strained.* His eyes were glazed-looking. She was worried. And then she said to herself, 'Oh, don't fuss! Nothing can happen. He can swim like a fish.'

They sat down to lunch together.

'Mummy,' he said, 'I can stay under water for two minutes — three minutes, at least.' It came bursting out of him.

'Can you, darling?' she said. 'Well, I shouldn't overdo it. I don't think you ought to swim any more today.'

She was ready for a battle of wills, but he gave in at once. It was no longer of the least importance to go to the bay.

Doris Lessing: Through the Tunnel 13

Glossary

The meanings given below are those which the words and phrases have as they occur in the story.

Page
3 *bay*: part of the coast where the land forms a semi-circle around the sea.
3 *contrition*: feeling sorry because he had not done what he felt was the right thing.
3 *unfailing impulse of contrition*: he always felt like that in this kind of situation.
4 *devotion*: loving care.
4 *promontories and inlets*: fingers of land sticking out into the sea and the small areas of water between them.
4 *cape*: like a promontory.
4 *at a stone's throw*: (*idiom.*) he stayed a short distance away from them.
4 *craving*: a very strong feeling of need.
4 *supplication*: asking very seriously for something from more powerful people.
5 *poised*: stood very still and carefully balanced.
5 *groping*: feeling for something with their hands.
5 *school*: group (usually, a large group of fish).
5 *stinging*: the water hurt his eyes.
5 *feat*: brave and difficult action.
6 *Bonjour!* etc.: (*French*) Hello! Thank you! Goodbye! Sir! Sir!
6 *waggled*: moved quickly up and down.
6 *his thighs*: the upper parts of his legs.
6 *fanged*: tooth-shaped.
6 *flushed*: pink.
6 *defiant and beseeching*: he didn't want his mother to have power over him but he also very much wanted her help.
7 *nagged and pestered*: kept on and on asking.
7 *sequins*: small bright decorations used on dresses.
7 *minute*: maɪnˈjuːt very small.
7 *sheer*: smooth and straight up; vertical.
7 *hugging it*: holding it against him with his arms.
7 *obstacle*: obstruction; something in the way.

14 *Innocence and Experience*

8 *anchor*: the rock he used to keep him in the right place.
8 *jammed*: fixed so he couldn't move them.
8 *clammy*: cold and wet.
8 *frond*: long, thin piece of seaweed.
8 *dizzy*: as if his head were turning round.
8 *torment*: terrible pain and suffering.
9 *incredulous*: didn't believe it could be true.
9 *throbbing*: the feeling of blood pumping.
10 *wriggling*: making small movements like a worm.
10 *rock-bound*: enclosed by rocks.
10 *no strain on his lungs*: he didn't find holding his breath difficult.
10 *pulsing*: similar to throbbing.
10 *slimy*: wet and slippery.
10 *tangle*: get caught and wrapped around.
10 *panicky*: with great fear and the need to escape danger.
10 *paled*: got lighter in colour.
11 *pounded*: throbbed strongly.
11 *feebly*: weakly, without strength.
11 *swelling*: growing.
11 *flung*: threw.
12 *was strained*: was tired from using a lot of nervous energy, but not relaxed.

Questions

1. Read the first paragraph of the story to see how, in its description of the two people and of the surroundings, it sums up the whole situation of Jerry and raises our interest in what is to follow. (p. 3)

   (a) Which two areas of the coast does Jerry look at when he stands on the path?
   (b) Jerry connects his mother with the crowded beach. What is the contrast between these associations and the rocky bay?
   (c) Why does his mother feel impatient with Jerry and worry over things he might secretly be thinking about?

Doris Lessing: Through the Tunnel 15

    (d) Why does he feel sorry for staying behind?
    (e) When he runs to catch up with his mother, what does he look back at and why does he think about it all morning?

2. What do the local boys mean to Jerry? Why is it so important to him that he should try to join them and what is the event that separates him from them so that he cries? (pp. 4—6)

    (a) What do the local boys look like and what sort of impression do you get of them from their behaviour?
    (b) Why was Jerry happy when he first joined them and how did he feel when he began diving with them?
    (c) What do the local boys do that Jerry fails to do?
    (d) How do they react when Jerry starts to behave in a silly way (like a foolish dog)?
    (e) Why does he feel 'hot shame' when they look at him?
    (f) Does Jerry stay with the local boys and join them as a friend?

3. How does Jerry prepare for his big test? Which things encourage him and which things might give him good reason to forget the whole idea?

    (a) What does he feel when he finds the entrance to the tunnel and looks into it? (p. 8)
    (b) What does he do about his breathing? (p. 8, p. 9)
    (c) What does he do while he is lying underwater on the sand? (p. 8)
    (d) What happens during the night following Jerry's first day of training and again two days before he is due to go home? (p. 8, p. 9)
    (e) Why does this make him afraid of what might happen in the tunnel? (p. 9)
    (f) Why does he feel he has to get through the tunnel? (p. 9)

4. Jerry's mother lays her head on his 'warm brown shoulder' (p. 12). This is the first time it is mentioned that Jerry is brown. Why is it mentioned at the end of the story?

    (a) In the first paragraph of the story we are told about

16 *Innocence and Experience*

> the mother's complexion. What does she mean to Jerry and how does he see himself in relation to her?
>
> (b) What colour are the local boys and what importance do they have for him? (pp. 4—6)
> (c) When Jerry's mother lays her head on his shoulder, does she act as she would to a child?
> (d) When she suggests that he looks pale, does Jerry accept her anxiety?
> (e) Jerry may *look* pale, but does he *feel* pale and helpless any more? Which group of people does he belong to now? Are these people children?

5. 'Water surged into his mouth; he choked, sank, came up.' (p. 6) How is this a summing up of Jerry's experience of life and his way of dealing with it?

   (a) What will Jerry prove to himself if he succeeds in swimming through the tunnel?
   (b) Is Jerry's meeting with the local boys a success? (p. 5)
   (c) Does he have to face unpleasant things in order to get through the tunnel?
   (d) There is an idiom in English for talking about a situation where there is only one chance or way of surviving: 'If I don't do this, *I'm sunk*.' How will Jerry feel if he cannot find the courage to swim through the tunnel?
   (e) Does he experience fear? Does he let himself be controlled by his fear? (See especially his experience when half-way through the tunnel.) (p. 10)

6. Jerry's mother *seems* very casual and even uninterested in him and what he does. Do you think she is really casual and uninterested?

   (a) What are her feelings in the first paragraph of the story?
   (b) Has Jerry any brothers or sisters and is his father alive? (p. 4) How might this affect his mother's attitude to him?
   (c) Why does Jerry's mother think she must be careful? (p. 3)

(d) When Jerry asks for the goggles, how does his mother reply to him and how does she look at him? What does the contrast show about her attitude? (pp. 6—7)

(e) When Jerry returns after his first day of preparation, his mother says only 'Did you enjoy yourself?' Why does she not show more interest? (p. 8)

(f) Look at the conversation between them at the end of the story and compare the mother's words with what we are told about her thoughts and feelings.

7. Did you find the account of Jerry's journey through the tunnel exciting? What is it about stories like this that a lot of people find fascinating? Can you think of other stories or films where people have to make similar difficult or dangerous journeys?

Susan Hill (1942—)

Susan Hill is a contemporary English writer whose novels and short stories have gained a wide readership over the last ten years. She won the Somerset Maugham Award in 1971 for 'I'm the King of the Castle' and the John Llewellyn Rhys Prize for 'The Albatross and Other Stories'. She has published a number of other novels and was elected a Fellow of the Royal Society of Literature in 1972. Susan Hill's stories are often about children and old people, whose experiences, frequently of a dark kind, she explores with great insight and sensitivity. 'The Badness Within Him' is published by Penguin in 'A Bit of Singing and Dancing' (1975).

The story

'The Badness Within Him' is concerned with a boy's struggle to come to terms with his feelings about himself and his family. These feelings he regards as wicked — the badness within him. The tension is maintained throughout the story, which builds up to a tragic event. This event breaks into the boy's isolation, bringing an opportunity for change and, perhaps, growth.

The Badness Within Him

The night before, he had knelt beside his bed and prayed for a storm, an urgent, hysterical prayer. But even while he prayed he had known that there could be no answer, because of the badness within him, a badness which was living and growing like a cancer. So that he was not surprised to draw back the curtains and see the pale, glittering* mist of another hot day. But he was angry. He did not want the sun and the endless stillness and brightness, the hard-edged shadows and the steely gleam of the sea. They came to this place every summer, they had been here, now, since the first of August, and they had one week more left. The sun had shone from the beginning. He wondered how he would bear it.*

At the breakfast table, Jess sat opposite to him and her hand kept moving up to rub at the sunburned skin which was peeling off her nose.

'Stop *doing* that.'

Jess looked up slowly. This year, for the first time, Col felt the difference in age between them, he saw that Jess was changing, moving away from him to join the adults. She was almost fourteen.

'What if the skin doesn't grow again? What then? You look awful enough now.'

She did not reply, only considered him for a long time, before returning her attention to the cereal plate. After a moment, her hand went up again to the peeling skin.

Col thought, I hate it here. I hate it. *I hate it.* And he clenched his fist* under cover of the table until the fingernails hurt him, digging into his palm. He had suddenly come to hate it, and the emotion frightened him. It was the reason why he had prayed for the storm, to break the pattern of long, hot, still days and waken the others out of their contentment, to change things. Now, everything was as it had always been in the past and he did not want the past, he wanted the future.

But the others were happy here, they slipped into the gentle, lazy routine of summer as their feet slipped into sandals, they

19

never grew bored or angry or irritable, never quarrelled with one another. For days now Col had wanted to quarrel.

How had he ever been able to bear it? And he cast about, in his frustration,* for some terrible event, as he felt the misery* welling up inside him at the beginning of another day.

I hate it here. He hated the house itself, the chintz curtains and covers bleached by the glare of the sun, and the crunch of sand like sugar spilled in the hall and along the tiled passages, the windows with peeling paint always open on to the garden, and the porch cluttered* with sandshoes and buckets and deck-chairs, the muddle and shabbiness of it all.*

They all came down to breakfast at different times, and ate slowly and talked of nothing, made no plans, for that was what the holiday was for, a respite* from plans and time-tables.

Fay pulled out the high chair and sat her baby down next to Col.

'You can help him with his egg.'

'Do I have to?'

Fay stared at him, shocked that anyone should not find her child desirable.

'Do help, Col, you know the baby can't manage by himself.'

'Col's got a black dog on his shoulder.'*

'Shut up.'

'A perfectly enormous, coal black, monster of a dog!'

He kicked out viciously* at his sister under the table. Jess began to cry.

'Now, Col, you are to apologize please.' His mother looked paler than ever, exhausted. Fay's baby dug fingers of toast down deeper and deeper into the yolk of egg.

'You hurt me, you hurt me.'

He looked out of the window. The sea was a thin, glistening* line. Nothing moved. Today would be the same as yesterday and all the other days — nothing would happen, nothing would change. He felt himself itching beneath his skin.

They had first come here when he was three years old. He remembered how great the distance had seemed as he jumped from rock to rock on the beach, how he had scarcely been able to stretch his leg across and balance. Then, he had stood for minute after minute feeling the damp ribs of sand under his feet. He had been enchanted* with everything. He and Jess had collected buckets full of sea creatures from the rock pools and put them into a glass aquarium in the scullery, though always the starfish and anemones and limpets died after a few, captive days. They had taken jam jars up on to West Cliff and walked along, at the hottest part of the day, looking for chrysalis on the grass stalks. The salt had dried in white tide marks around their brown legs, and Col had reached down and rubbed some off with his finger and then licked it. In the sun lounge the moths and butterflies had swollen and cracked open their frail, papery coverings and crept out like babies from the womb, and he and Jess had sat up half the night by the light of moon or candle, watching them.

And so it had been every year and often, in winter or windy spring in London, he remembered it all, the smell of the sunlit house and the feeling of the warm sea lapping against his thighs* and the line of damp woollen bathing shorts outside the open back door. It was another world, but it was still there, and when every summer came they would return to it, things would be the same.

Yet now, he wanted to do some violence in this house, he wanted an end to everything. He was afraid of himself.

'Col's got a black dog on his shoulder!'

So he left them and went for a walk on his own, over the track beside the gorse bushes and up on to the coarse grass of the sheep field behind West Cliff. The mist was rolling away, the sea was white-gold at the edges, creaming back. On the far side of the field there were poppies.*

He lay down and pressed his face and hands into the warm turf until he could smell the soil beneath and gradually, he felt the warmth of the sun on his back and it soothed him.*

In the house, his mother and sisters left the breakfast table and wandered upstairs to find towels and sunhats and books, content that this day should be the same as all the other days, wanting the summer to last. And later, his father would join them for the weekend, coming down on the train from London, he would discard* the blue city suit and emerge, hairy and thickly fleshed, to lie on a rug and snore and play with Fay's baby, rounding off* the family circle.

By eleven it was hotter than it had been all summer, the dust rose in soft clouds when a car passed down the lane to the village, and did not settle again, and the leaves of the hedges were mottled and dark, the birds went quiet. Col felt his own anger like a pain tightening around his head. He went up to the house and lay on his bed trying to read, but the room was airless and the sunlight fell in a straight, hard beam across his bed and on to the printed page, making his eyes hurt.

When he was younger he had liked this room, he had sometimes dreamed of it when he was in London. He had collected shells and small pebbles and laid them out in careful piles, and hung up a bladder-wrack* on a nail by the open window, had brought books from home about fossils and shipwrecks and propped them on top of the painted wooden chest. But now it felt too small, it stifled him, *it was a childish room, a pale, dead room in which nothing ever happened and nothing would change.

After a while he heard his father's taxi come up the drive.

'Col, do watch what you're doing near the baby, you'll get sand in his eyes.'

'Col, if you want to play this game with us, do, but otherwise go away, if you can't keep still, you're just spoiling it.'

'Col, why don't you build a sandcastle or something?'

He stood looking down at them all, at his mother and Fay playing cards in the shade of the green parasol, and his father lying on his back, his bare, black-haired chest shiny with oil and his nostrils flaring in and out as he breathed, at Jess, who had begun to build the sandcastle for the baby, instead of him. She had her hair tied back in bunches and the freckles* had come out even more thickly across her cheekbones, she might have been eleven years old. But she was almost fourteen, she had gone away from him.

'Col, don't kick the sand like that, it's flying everywhere. Why don't you go and have a swim? Why can't you find something to do? I do so dislike you just hovering over us like that.'

Jess had filled a small bucket with water from the rock pool, and now she bent down and began to pour it carefully into the moat.* It splashed on to her bare feet and she wriggled her toes.

Fay's baby bounced up and down with interest and pleasure in the stream of water and the crenellated golden castle.

Col kicked again more forcefully. The clods of sand hit the tower of the castle sideways, and, as it fell, crumbled the edges off the other towers and broke open the surrounding wall, so that everything toppled into the moat, clouding the water.

Jess got to her feet, scarlet in the face, ready to hit out at him.

'I hate you. *I hate you.*'

'Jess . . .'

'He wants to spoil everything, look at him, he doesn't want anyone else to enjoy themselves, he just wants to sulk and . . . I hate him.'

Col thought, I am filled with evil, there is no hope for me. For he felt himself completely taken over by the badness within him.

'*I hate you.*'

He turned away from his sister's wild face and her mouth which opened and shut over and over again to shout her rejection of him,* turned away from them all and began to walk towards the caves at the far side of the cove. Above them were the cliffs.

Three-quarters of the way up there was a ledge around which the gannets and kittiwakes* nested. He had never climbed up as high as this before. There were tussocks of grass, dried and bleached bone-pale by the sea winds, and he clung on to them and to the bumps of chalky rock. Flowers grew, pale wild scabious and cliff buttercups, and when he rested, he touched his face to them. Above his head, the sky was enamel blue. The sea birds watched him with eyes like beads. As he climbed higher, the wash of the sea and the voices of those on the beach receded. When he reached the ledge, he got his breath and then sat down cautiously, legs dangling over the edge. There was just enough room for him. The surface of the cliff was hot on his back. He was not at all afraid.

His family were like insects down on the sand, little shapes of colour dotted about at random. Jess was a pink shape, the parasol was bottle-glass green, Fay and Fay's baby were yellow. For most of the time they were still, but once they all clustered around the parasol to look at something and then broke away again, so that it was like a dance. The other people on the beach were quite

24 Innocence and Experience

separate, each family kept itself to itself. Out beyond the curve of the cliff the beach lay like a ribbon bounded by the tide, which did not reach as far as the cove except in the storms of winter. They had never been here during the winter.

When Col opened his eyes again his head swam* for a moment. Everything was the same. The sky was thin and clear. The sun shone. If he had gone to sleep he might have tipped over and fallen forwards. The thought did not frighten him.

But all was not the same, for now he saw his father had left the family group and was paddling down towards the sea. The black hairs curled up the backs of his legs and the soles of his feet were brownish pink as they turned up one after the other.

Col said, do I like my father? And thought about it. And did not know.

Fay's baby was crawling after him, its lemon-coloured behind stuck up in the air.

Now, Col half-closed his eyes, so that air and sea and sand shimmered, merging together.

Now, he felt rested, no longer angry, he felt above it all.

Now, he opened his eyes again and saw his father striding into the water, until it reached up to his chest: then he flopped onto his belly and floated for a moment, before beginning to swim.

Col thought, perhaps I am ill and *that* is the badness within me.

But if he had changed, the others had changed too. Since Fay had married and had the baby and gone to live in Berkshire, she was different, she fussed* more, was concerned with the details of things, she spoke to them all a trifle impatiently. And his mother was so languid.* And Jess — Jess did not want his company.

Now he saw his father's dark head bobbing up and down quite a long way out to sea, but as he watched, sitting on the high cliff ledge in the sun, the bobbing stopped — began again — an arm came up and waved, though as if it were uncertain of its direction.

Col waved back.

The sun was burning the top of his head.

Fay and Fay's baby and Jess had moved in around the parasol again, their heads were bent together. Col thought, we will never be the same with one another, the ties of blood* make no difference, we are separate people now. And then he felt afraid of such truth. Father's waving stopped abruptly, he bobbed and disappeared, bobbed up again.

The sea was as still as glass.

Col saw that his father was drowning.

In the end, a man from the other side of the beach went running down to the water's edge and another to where the family were grouped around the parasol. Col looked at the cliff, falling away at his feet. He closed his eyes and turned around slowly and then got down on his hands and knees and began to feel for a foothold, though not daring to look. His head was hot and throbbing.*

By the time he reached the bottom, they were bringing his father's body. Col stood in the shadow of the cliff and shivered* and smelled the dank, cave smell behind him. His mother and Fay and Jess stood in a line, very erect, like Royalty at the Cenotaph,* and in Fay's arms the baby was still as a doll.

Everyone else kept away, though Col could see that they made half-gestures, raised an arm or turned a head, occasionally took an uncertain step forward, before retreating again.

Eventually he wondered if they had forgotten about him. The men dripped water off their arms and shoulders as they walked and the sea ran off the body, too, in a thin, steady stream.

Nobody spoke to him about the cliff climb. People only spoke of baths and hot drinks and telephone messages, scarcely looking at one another as they did so, and the house was full of strangers moving from room to room.

In bed, he lay stiffly under the tight sheets and looked towards the window where the moon shone. He thought, it is my fault. I prayed for some terrible happening and the badness within me made it come about. I am punished. For this was a change greater than he could have imagined.

When he slept he dreamed of drowning, and woke early, just at dawn. Outside the window, a dove grey mist muffled everything. He felt the cold linoleum under his feet and the dampness in his nostrils.* When he reached the bottom of the stairs he saw at once that the door of the sun parlour was closed. He stood for a moment outside, listening to the creaking of the house, imagining all of them in their beds, his mother lying alone. He was afraid. He turned the brass doorknob and went slowly in.

There were windows on three sides of the room, long and uncurtained, with a view of the sea, but now there was only the fog pressing up against the panes, the curious stillness. The floor was polished and partly covered with rush matting and in the ruts of this the sand of all the summer past had gathered and lay, soft and gritty, the room smelled of seaweed. On the walls, the sepia photographs of his great-grandfather the Captain, and his naval friends and their ships. He had always liked this room. When he was small, he had sat here with his mother on warm, August evenings, drinking his mug of milk, and the smell of stocks* came in to them from the open windows. The deckchairs had always been in a row outside on the terrace, empty at the end of the day. He stepped forward.

They had put his father's body on the trestle,* dressed in a shirt and covered with a sheet and a rug. His head was bare* and lay on a cushion, and the hands, with the black hair over their backs, were folded together. Now, he was not afraid. His father's skin was oddly pale and shiny. He stared, trying to feel some sense of loss and sorrow. He had watched his father drown, though for a long time he had not believed it, the water had been so entirely calm. Later, he had heard them talking about a heart attack, and then he had understood better why this strong barrel of a man, down that day from the City, should have been so suddenly sinking, sinking.

The fog horn* sounded outside. Then, he knew that the change had come, knew that the long, hot summer was at an end, and that his childhood had ended too, that they would never come to this house again. He knew, finally, the power of the badness within him and because of that, standing close to his father's body, he wept.

Glossary

The meanings given below are those which the words and phrases have as they occur in the story.

Page
19 *glittering*: shining brightly.
19 *bear it*: stand it, tolerate it or put up with it.
19 *clenched his fist*: held his fingers tightly bent together.
20 *frustration*: anger because he didn't feel free.
20 *misery*: great unhappiness.
20 *cluttered*: filled untidily.
20 *the shabbiness of it all*: everything that surrounded Col seemed to him stale, soiled and dull.
20 *respite*: pleasant change from something unpleasant.
20 *Col's got a black dog on his shoulder*: (*idiom*.) He's in a bad mood.
20 *viciously*: aggressively, wanting to hurt.
20 *glistening*: shining.
21 *he had been enchanted*: he had found it very interesting and exciting.
21 *lapping against his thighs*: moving gently against the upper parts of his legs.
21 *poppies*: red flowers.
21 *soothed him*: calmed him; made him feel relaxed.
21 *discard*: take off and put away as not needed.
21 *rounding off*: completing.
22 *bladder-wrack*: a kind of seaweed.
22 *stifled him*: made him feel he couldn't breathe.
22 *freckles*: spots of brown on the skin.
22 *moat*: water around the sandcastle.
23 *rejection of him*: she behaved as if she didn't love him and wasn't interested in him.
23 *gannets and kittiwakes*: kinds of sea bird.
24 *his head swam*: he felt faint, as if his head were turning round.
24 *fussed*: worried about little, unimportant things.
24 *languid*: tired; without energy.
24 *ties of blood*: the emotional connections between people of one family.

28 *Innocence and Experience*

25 *throbbing*: he could feel the blood pumping through his head.
25 *shivered*: his body shook as though he were cold.
25 *like Royalty at the Cenotaph*: as a member of the Royal Family stands at a ceremony (very still and upright). The Cenotaph is a war memorial in London and there is a ceremony there once a year.
25 *nostrils*: openings of his nose.
26 *stocks*: a kind of garden flower.
26 *trestle*: stand for placing a coffin on. (Coffin: box for a dead body.)
26 *bare*: uncovered.
26 *fog horn*: used to warn ships by sound when fog or mist makes it impossible to see far.

Questions

1. Most people hope for sun during a summer holiday. Col hoped for a storm. Why? (p. 19)

    (a) This year, does he still enjoy being in the familiar holiday surroundings?
    (b) What has the weather been like during the holiday?
    (c) Does Col want his life to continue in the same way?

2. 'He wanted the future.' (p. 19) Why do you think Col longed so much for change?

    (a) Is he enjoying his family's company?
    (b) Who is Fay? Is she a child or an adult?
    (c) How did Col get on with his sister Jess when he was very young? (p. 21)
    (d) What is happening to Jess?
    (e) Who are the other people around Col? Does he feel close to any of them?
    (f) Are the other members of the family happy? How does Col feel about that? (pp. 19–20)

3. 'He was afraid of himself.' (p. 21) What does Col see to make him afraid of himself?

Susan Hill: The Badness Within Him

- (a) At the beginning of the story, what had Col done on the previous night?
- (b) What kind of change does Col really want? Does he think of pleasant change?
- (c) How does he feel about helping Fay's baby and what does he do to Jess? (p. 20)
- (d) Does he have loving feelings for his family? (e.g. p. 19, p. 21)
- (e) What sorts of feelings does his family think he should have for them?

4. What sorts of things do you think make Col think he is 'filled with evil'? (p. 23) Make use of your study of the previous questions to answer this one and number 5, below.

5. Why does Col go away from the others and climb up the cliff? (p. 23)

6. 'the ties of blood make no difference, we are separate people now.' (p. 24) How does this remark help us understand Col's situation and the way he sees it?

   - (a) How did Col and Jess get on before and how do they get on now?
   - (b) Does he look forward to the arrival of his father? (p. 21)
   - (c) Is Fay interested in him as a brother? (p. 20)
   - (d) Is Col's mother loving and affectionate to him?
   - (e) Do you think Col felt secure as part of the family when he was younger?
   - (f) Does he still feel part of the family?

7. 'Col waved back.' (p. 24) This is a terrible sentence, partly because the father was in fact drowning. Can you think of another way in which it is terrible?

   - (a) Waving is a friendly way of greeting somebody. Col waves *back* to his father. What does he think his father has just done and why?
   - (b) Has his father noticed him and was he greeting him in a friendly way?

30 *Innocence and Experience*

   (c) Are there any points in the story where Col and his father communicate with each other?

8. Susan Hill uses descriptions of the weather to help build up a picture of Col's mood. Can you find some examples?

   (a) How are the shadows and the sea described in the first paragraph?

   (b) How do the others react to the weather and how does their mood make Col feel? (pp. 19–20)

   (c) As the weather gets hotter, how does Col's mood change?

   (d) What is the weather like on the morning after his father's death? (p. 25, p. 26)

9. Col remembers earlier times at certain points in the story. Find some of these and see how they are used.

   (a) What has just happened when Col thinks back to earlier holidays when he was younger and happier? (p. 20)

   (b) Col thinks about the beach, the house and the company of his sister Jess. Were they pleasant things for him then?

   (c) How does he feel in his bedroom? Has he always felt that way about it?

   (d) What is said about the room in which the father's body is placed? (p. 26)

10. At the end of the story, Col gets the change he has been longing for. How does it make him feel and think about himself and his life?

   (a) Do the other members of the family take any notice of Col when he joins them on the beach at the time of his father's death? (p. 25)

   (b) What does Col think was the cause of his father's death? What thoughts does he have when he goes to bed that night? (p. 25)

   (c) Did he realize what was happening when he watched his father from the cliff? (p. 24, p. 26)

Susan Hill: The Badness Within Him 31

- (d) Does he begin to understand the real reason for his father's death?
- (e) Does this understanding make him feel any differently about himself (i) as a child, separate from all the others; (ii) as being responsible for his father's death?
- (f) Will the family return for another holiday?

* * * * *

1. In both stories, the boys spend very important times alone. Compare the ways Col and Jerry use these times.

2. Both boys are hoping for change. What differences are there in the ways they try to bring about these changes? Look at the kinds of change they hope for. Are these changes (i) in themselves; (ii) in their environment and other people; (iii) in their relationships?

3. Both boys experience fear. How does each react to his fear? For Jerry see, for instance, his first entrance into the tunnel (p. 8); his decision (p. 8); when he thinks about the possibility of octopuses (p. 8); his reactions when he realizes he is only half way through (p. 11). For Col see, for instance, p. 19. What is he frightened of, and how does he hope to make things different? See also p. 21. What — or who — is Col frightened of, and where does he go because of this?

4. In both stories the sea plays a big part. Look at the way it is described in each story and the different ways the two boys experience the presence of the sea.
   - (a) Does Col go swimming? Does he take much notice of the sea as something interesting or enjoyable?
   - (b) Here are two groups of words, one for each story, which are used to describe the sea. Which group belongs to which story and how do these words help us understand how each boy experienced the sea?

32 *Innocence and Experience*

> (i) crisping, lapping, purple, darker blue, luminous, gleaming, warm, cold, sparkled, flaked silver, clear jewel green, darkness.
>
> (ii) steely gleam, thin, glistening line, still as glass.

5. What do you think Jerry's and Col's lives will be like after the changes that take place in them? Which of the two boys do you feel you understand better or sympathize with more? What sorts of things have made you feel fear and how have you dealt with those situations?

Discovery

Denys Val Baker (1917–)

A contemporary British writer who has lived for many years in Cornwall, the south-western corner of England and an area that has a strong literary tradition of its own. He has written several autobiographical books and many short stories, a number of which have been broadcast by the B.B.C. The last collection of his stories to be published is entitled 'The Woman and the Engine Driver'. He has also edited 'Cornish Short Stories' (Penguin) and 'The Discovery' is included in that collection.

The story

Luke and his younger brother are on holiday in Cornwall. They discover a beautiful lake and start to think of it as their own. When Elizabeth and her father arrive on the scene, however, changes and discoveries take place that affect them all.

The Discovery

I can remember the clay pool now as vividly as the first morning when Luke and I climbed through the ruins of an old Cornish mine house and followed a path up the steep, moss-covered slope — and there, falling away from us into vast, silent space, lay the shimmering blue, unbelievably bright blue surface.

We were staying with our parents at a cottage just outside Nancledra, in the Penwith Hills above St Ives. Everywhere around the hills rose up bleak* and austere,* more often than not crowned by some forlorn finger of a mine chimney, rearing impotently against the ageless sky. The mines were long since silent, the shafts filled with water, and the crumbling ruins of their machine heads* merely served to emphasize the strange atmosphere of past.

It was a country ripe for exploration by two youngsters glad to escape from London smog* for a while, and most mornings Luke and I slipped away, adventure bound. Luke was my elder brother, nearly fifteen, three years older than I, with an air of native authority to which I was glad to succumb.* He was tall and fair, with a boyish charm that was just beginning to set with a touch of manliness: beside him I felt an inadequate, uncouth* schoolboy. And needless to say I worshipped him with the peculiarly concentrated devotion that younger brothers have at that tender age.

It was Luke, naturally, who took the lead on our expeditions. Luke who said, 'Let's see if we can find that old Roman village at Chyauster.' Or, 'What's Castle-en-Dinas? Let's go and find out.' And we'd set off on the trail, Luke remembering to be a very grown-up fifteen frowning on too much horseplay* — myself, at least secretly, imagining us as some scouting party of ancient Britons, or maybe the current equivalent of Davy Crockett.*

But whatever our attitudes, I think both of us were always impressed, and often awed,* by the magnificent solitude and mystery of those Cornish moors,* so impregnated with* weird* memories and suggestions of the past. It was not difficult to feel, as I have since read that George Meredith* wrote, that in Cornwall

36 *Discovery*

the past was always at your elbow. We always felt that at any moment something strange, perhaps supernatural, could happen.

It was rather like that with our discovery of the blue clay pool. We had heard one or two of the farmers talk about it, but only casually. Somehow it did not seem altogether real. For us it was part of the general mythology, a place that existed — somewhere.

And then, suddenly, there it was spread out before our astonished eyes all in its delicate and transparent* beauty. Anyone who has walked among mountains and come upon a lake will know the strange excitement of seeing enclosed water high up, many miles away from its natural home of the sea. But lake water is usually a rather dull grey or green: this was quite different, this was a huge dazzling splash of glistening blue — indeed, it might have been the sea itself. What's more, all around the edge there were sloping white sands, just as if there was a real beach.

I can remember how Luke and I just stood at the top for quite a time, staring. Perhaps neither of us had ever seen anything quite so beautiful, and we wanted to savour it to the full.*

Then we awoke to reality, and with wild cries of delight we charged down the slope, and across the wide white sands, to the very edge of this secret and mysterious blue sea.

'Look, Luke,' I cried, pointing in wonder. 'You can see right to the bottom!'

And indeed, the water was crystal clear, pure and innocent. How long had it lain silently there? How many hundreds of years ago had this pool begun as a tiny trickle, rising higher and higher as the nearby clay pit deepened, gradually enveloping more and more of the land? We could not know: the blue pool stared blandly* up at us, and we knew we could never know all its secrets.

But at least it gave us a new, marvellous playground. For at least half the way round we could follow the sandy edge before it became lost in a mass of tangled undergrowth. There were several bends in the 'coast' and round each one we found new excitements. At one point a small red stream trickled out of the hillside, forming a tiny tributary running into the pool: we spent hours damming it up with broken pieces of rock. In another part a tree had, weirdly, grown out over the water. We climbed catlike along the swaying branch, until we could lie there staring down into a depth of water that seemed unfathomable.*

'Ugh! I wouldn't like to fall down there,' said Luke.

But there was no real fear behind his remark. Somehow the blue pool wasn't like that. It was strange, it was even ghostly at times, and it certainly seemed a world of its own — but it was never sinister or evil, like some parts of Cornwall can be. It was always, for us both, a magical kingdom of its own, our blue heaven.

By tacit consent,* Luke and I said very little about the pool. It was our own secret, we wanted to keep it for ourselves, and so we did — from our parents anyway. We weren't able to get there every day, of course, but usually we did — sometimes quite early in the morning, and on one or two occasions in the evening, when the fading sunlight gave the pool an added charm.

I suppose in the uncomplicated way of children we came to look on the pool as our own. After all, hadn't we discovered it like explorers of old, that morning when we breasted the hill? I really think we must have felt rather like that, possessive and proud.

And so we were quite upset one afternoon when we found our kingdom invaded by intruders. We watched angrily, sheltered by a tree. There they were as bold as brass,* rambling along the far side — a tall, thickset man with a walking stick, and a young girl.

We glared suspiciously, willing them to go away and leave us in peace. But they did nothing of the kind; indeed after a while the man with the stick sat down on a boulder* and began unpacking a packet of sandwiches, and the little girl went and sat by him and they settled down to a meal.

Somewhat self-consciously, Luke and I came down on the beach. Usually we would gambol about* or chase each other, or climb up and down the rocky parts. Somehow, now it was impossible. We felt conscious all the time of the strangers. Their sharing of our secret took away its pleasure.

It was only when they got up to go, and came along past where we were seated, rather disconsolately* throwing stones into the pool, that we felt our depression lifting. As they came along, out of curiosity we could not help looking. The man, to us, looked quite old. He had frizzy* grey hair and a lined face, and leaned heavily on his stick, walking with a limp. As he came abreast of us, he paused and eyed us keenly from under bushy eyebrows.

'Ha!' he said, in a booming* voice. 'Captain Morgan and Captain Kidd, I presume?' He turned and stabbed his stick out across the pool. 'Better look out, there's a Government frigate* on the horizon.'

And then, with another 'Ha!' and a 'Ho!' he went on. And as he did so, just behind him, we were both conscious of the girl. She wore a dress of almost the same colour as the pool, and against it she shone with a delicate radiance of her own. She had dark hair done up in pigtails, hanging over her back, and I can remember that her blue eyes were large and solemn, as they looked at us. I didn't feel there was anything special about her. She was just a girl, older than I, maybe about Luke's age.

But Luke, I knew, felt different. It wasn't anything he said, just something in the way he looked at the girl, and the way, once or twice, after she had walked on, clinging* to her father's hand, that she cast a backward glance. Just something — something in the air as you might say.

'Well, I'm glad they're gone,' I said, irritable from my awareness of Luke's interest.

He watched them go, up the hill and out of sight. His face looked vacant, as if his thoughts were far away.

'Yes,' he said. He picked up a large stone and threw it far out into the lake, watching the ripples travel all the way back to the shore.

'I wonder who they are?' said Luke.

We found out soon enough. Somehow, whether by some accident or design* I never knew, they were there again the next day. This time, in the way these things happen, we began talking. The man with the stick and the booming voice probably began it, with his jokes about pirates. I rather liked him. With his frizzy hair and broad shoulders he reminded me of a great bear, and he had about him that warmth and friendliness which, rightly or wrongly, I have always associated with bears.

Mind you, he was a very talkative bear. He enjoyed the act of talking itself. His voice seemed to well up from deep down and fairly boom out, echoing and re-echoing over the pool. He had a curious way of talking in fantasy, too. Just as he had immediately labelled us as pirates, so he had a way of referring to ordinary things and events, and making them sound quite extraordinary.

'That's why I like living in Cornwall, boy,' he said to me once. 'Feel at home here, you see. Ha!'

His daughter, Elizabeth, was far less forthcoming.* At first she stayed very close to her father, staring at us with those round, wondering eyes. Indeed it was he, with his bluff* laugh and a careless wave of his walking stick, who first encouraged her out of her shyness.

'C'mmun,* girl. You needn't be afraid. They're only children like yourself. Why don't you go and play?'

It wasn't as easy as that. Elizabeth, rather like her name suggested, was one of the serious, quiet types. And I guess Mr Slater, that was her father's name, understood her well enough, for he led her along very slowly into our company, not forcing or bullying. He was very fond of his daughter, we could see that. We learned later that his wife had recently died, and he was bringing Elizabeth up on his own.

I suppose I was antagonistic to* her from the beginning. Or suspicious, maybe. I suspected that faintly ethereal* appearance. I suspected those round, innocent eyes. I distrusted that shyness, that gentle withdrawal. In my bones I knew, withal,* she was of the stuff that women are made.

Gradually, we began playing together, the three of us. Most afternoons we would come up and find Mr Slater and Elizabeth already there, waiting, and then we would go off and play, leaving Mr Slater leaning against a rock, staring out upon the water.

We played — but it wasn't the same as before, not for me. We still went exploring, and climbed out on the tree, and made up adventures. But none of them were quite the same. Upon them all, even if she was not aware of it, Elizabeth imposed a curious, soft feminine restraint.* Once or twice I saw Luke helping her, across a stream, over the tree branch — grinning quickly, an arm holding her elbow. Girls, I thought. Girls . . .

Sometimes, in that mood, I would wander away on my own, perhaps down to where Mr Slater sat. I suppose I went for the entertainment. I liked the way he brought out startling images and created fantastic situations. He was an author, apparently, and though that meant very little to me, I gathered from the way in which Elizabeth breathed the word that it was something distinguished.*

'He sits in his room every morning, writing. He's written *eight* books,' said Elizabeth importantly.

Luke whistled.

'He must be very clever.'

But I looked at them both irritably, for I knew they were just saying words — they didn't really *feel* Mr Slater's cleverness deep down, like I did. I didn't care how many books he'd written, but I knew he was somebody special.

'Look at that seagull, boy,' he'd say, poking his stick. 'More beautiful than all your airplanes. And not factory made, eh?'

'Sky's like a painting today, boy. Can't you just see some fellow stick on the paints — all crimson and orange and indigo. There, dab-dab-dab!'

And somehow, under Mr Slater's wandering gaze, my own eyes began to open upon the world proper, upon all the topsy turvy* inexplicable* wonderful things that went on in the world.

But all the time, Luke and Elizabeth would be playing, down by the beach, maybe making up games on their own.

And then one afternoon we were surprised to see Elizabeth come on her own. She said her father had decided to lie down for a rest. He might come along later.

I can remember her that afternoon. She wore a bright green blouse and a red skirt; somehow she looked much older than usual, much more grown up.

And, yes, it was odd, but she seemed different from other times. There was no doubt about it. It was as if the absence of her father had produced a liberating* effect. Perhaps, secretly, she had always wanted to be free of that guiding hand — had really not wanted the familiar figure to shelter behind.

I don't know. I couldn't fathom* it then and I don't suppose I would now. I only knew that this was a different girl and that Luke felt the same, too, because he kept staring at her puzzledly.* That is, until she turned round eyes upon him and stared back.

Then he did something I couldn't ever remember seeing before. He blushed. Luke, my elder brother, blushed.

We all went along the white sandy beach. It was a perfect afternoon: the sun scorching down, the sands hot on our feet. It was the sort of afternoon when you could think of nothing really except how wonderful it would be to dive deep down into some cold clear water.

'I know,' said Elizabeth suddenly. 'Why don't we bathe?'

Luke and I both looked at her remembering that on past occasions any such suggestions had been vetoed.* But we didn't need to see the unfamiliar glint* in her eyes to realize that the obstacle* to the suggestion, Mr Slater, was for the first time missing.

'You never know,' he would have said, shaking his great head gravely,* 'Quick sands* in the middle . . . very deep . . . mustn't take chances at your age.'

But though we would have obeyed him, we knew in our hearts that the dangers weren't important. We were young and healthy. We could manage. It had always been a great tantalization.*

'All right,' said Luke suddenly. 'I'm game.'*

'Me, too,' I said, liking the idea at least, even if it was Elizabeth's.

Luke hesitated. 'We haven't any costumes.'*

Elizabeth hardly seemed to hear him. Already she had turned away and was stepping over the rocks towards a patch of grass.

'We'll go in without.' She half-turned and looked back, and it seemed to me there was a secret mischief in her eyes, all for Luke. 'Promise you won't look until I'm in the water?'

We promised, and resolutely turned our backs. Once I essayed* a quick peep,* and Luke smacked me on the shoulder, quite hard. I looked at him in surprise, and saw that his face was curiously set.

'You mustn't do that,' he said. 'You *mustn't*.'

Suddenly there was a whirl* of air and noise and then a frothing sound, and then a final splash, and a moment later Elizabeth called out, from a long way away.

'All right — come on in. It's lovely, really lovely.'

We undressed quickly, and ran into the waters of our familiar magical blue pool. How cool and refreshing they were, how soft and gentle to the touch — what rapture* to plunge out of the sun's heat into such exquisite* coolness.

We splashed about for a while, and then began swimming around. So far we had not gone out of our depth, but now Luke proposed swimming across to a rock jutting out on the opposite side. It wasn't far, but I knew I couldn't do it.

Luke knew, too, and gave me stern admonishments* not to try. Then he and Elizabeth, who were both good swimmers, set off side by side.

I stood and watched them going, their bodies white, and to me almost transparent in the clear water. Suddenly I felt as if I were watching two strangers, perhaps creatures of the pool. Their white limbs,* so much longer than mine, seemed to merge into the eternal blueness of the pool. Soon I could only see their two heads bobbing* from side to side — and hear from afar the laughter of their voices as they shouted to one another.

Then, suddenly, I felt unutterably* lonely. I felt I did not want to stay in the water any longer, indeed I felt rather foolish. Quickly I turned and ran back to the bank, and put on some clothes. Then, almost casually, I turned, and saw Mr Slater.

He had just arrived, and was standing by the rock where he usually sat, leaning on his stick, and staring across the water. Following his gaze, I saw that he was watching his daughter Elizabeth and Luke. They had reached the rock and were clinging on, and lazily splashing one another. It was too far away to see their faces, but we could hear quite clearly their laughter. It seemed to rise up out of the blue pool, as clear and definite, as positive of meaning as the sunshine itself. There was no mistaking the tone of their laughter — no mistaking the sound of their happiness.

As I watched it seemed to me that Mr Slater, the great bear, almost crumpled up.* I saw his shoulders sag,* and his whole body seemed to lean with almost unbearable weight upon his walking stick. I felt the utter* poignancy* of the moment. And then, slowly, he turned and began walking away, back the way he had come.

'Mr Slater!' I called. 'Mr Slater!'

He didn't stop, but I ran after him and caught him up along

the path lined with brambles and blackberry bushes. He didn't say anything, because I realize now he was too full of emotion. For that matter, so was I. We walked along in silence all the way back to his cottage, and it wasn't till we reached the broad stone porchway that he turned and put a hand on my head.

'Ah, well, boy, don't worry — you'll grow up one day, too.'

I didn't know what he meant really then, but I do now. I went back to the blue pool the other day. It lay cool and shimmering in the midday heat, and as I lay and feasted my eyes* on its quiet beauty, I couldn't help remembering. I guess Mr Slater and I were both mourning* the same thing. Something to do with the magic of a blue pool on a summer's day, of youth growing up, of love blossoming.* But I guess if I'm honest there was something else too — something to do with a girl with dark pigtails and round, questioning eyes — and how for the rest of my life a part of me would always wish it had been me, and not Luke, who swam with her across the unknown, virginal* waters of the blue pool.

Glossary

The meanings given below are those which the words and phrases have as they occur in the story.

Page
35 *bleak*: bare; with few plants or trees.
35 *austere*: hard; ungentle.
35 *machine heads*: mining buildings and machinery at ground level.
35 *smog*: mixture of fog and smoke and exhaust from cars.
35 *succumb*: agree to; give way to.
35 *uncouth*: awkward and rough.
35 *horseplay*: rough, noisy play.
35 *Davy Crockett*: (1786—1836) early American frontiersman and national hero.
35 *awed*: full of respect, almost fearful respect.
35 *moors*: wild, open land.
35 *impregnated with*: filled with.
35 *weird*: strange.
35 *George Meredith*: (1828—1909) British poet and novelist.
36 *transparent*: clear; can be seen through.
36 *to savour it to the full*: to appreciate it completely.
36 *blandly*: quietly; gently.
37 *unfathomable*: so deep that the bottom could not be reached.
37 *By tacit consent*: understanding without putting into words.
37 *as bold as brass*: (*idiom.*) without respect.
37 *boulder*: large rounded stone.
37 *gambol about*: play happily; skipping and jumping.
37 *disconsolately*: unhappily; as though having lost something.
37 *frizzy*: tightly curled.
38 *booming*: deep and powerful.
38 *frigate*: old-fashioned sailing ship; previously a warship.
38 *clinging*: holding tightly.
38 *by some accident or design*: by chance or on purpose.
39 *forthcoming*: willing to talk.
39 *bluff*: rough but kind.
39 *c'mmun*: (*coll. abbr.*) Come on.
39 *antagonistic to*: against; hostile to.

39 *ethereal*: light; delicate; spiritual.
39 *withal*: (*archaic*) moreover; as well.
39 *restraint*: holding back; power of preventing someone from doing as they wish.
40 *distinguished*: important; that separates someone from other people.
40 *topsy turvy*: confusing; upside down.
40 *inexplicable*: cannot be explained.
40 *liberating*: setting free.
40 *fathom*: understand.
40 *puzzledly*: finding it difficult to understand.
41 *vetoed*: not allowed.
41 *glint*: bright look, gleam or flash.
41 *obstacle*: thing that stops someone doing something.
41 *gravely*: seriously.
41 *quick sands*: sands which suck people etc. down.
41 *tantalization*: thing that is desired.
41 *I'm game*: I'm willing.
41 *costumes*: swimming clothes.
41 *essayed*: tried; attempted.
41 *peep*: short look taken through curiosity.
41 *whirl*: quick movement.
42 *rapture*: great delight; ecstasy.
42 *exquisite*: highly pleasurable.
42 *stern admonishments*: strict warnings.
42 *limbs*: arms and legs.
42 *bobbing*: moving up and down.
42 *unutterably*: unspeakably.
42 *crumpled up*: became smaller as though crushed by unhappiness.
42 *sag*: move down as though under pressure.
42 *utter*: complete; total.
42 *poignancy*: deep and disturbing feeling.
43 *feasted my eyes*: looked with extreme pleasure.
43 *mourning*: feeling of great unhappiness as when someone dies.
43 *blossoming*: developing and growing (like flowers).
43 *virginal*: natural; pure.

46 *Discovery*

Questions

1. What is special to the boys about the Cornish countryside and the pool?

    (a) Are the boys from Cornwall? (p. 35)
    (b) What does the younger boy secretly feel about his exploration of the countryside? (p. 35)
    (c) What does the writer say is special about any lake in a mountainous district? (p. 36)
    (d) Why is this particular lake even more impressive?
    (e) '... the blue pool stared blandly up at us, and we knew we could never know all its secrets' (p. 36) What secrets?
    (f) Is the pool frightening? (p. 37)
    (g) Why are the boys so upset when 'intruders' come along? (p. 37)

2. In what ways are Luke's and his brother's attitudes to Elizabeth different?

    (a) What are the ages of the three children in the story? (p. 35, p. 38)
    (b) What does the younger boy think of his brother? (p. 35)
    (c) Why is the younger boy 'irritable' after Elizabeth has passed them for the first time? (p. 38)
    (d) 'I suppose I was antagonistic to her from the beginning.' (p. 39) Why is the younger brother antagonistic to Elizabeth?
    (e) Would you say Luke or his brother understands Elizabeth better?

3. What changes and developments occur between the characters of the story?

    (a) The characters form pairs at the beginning of the story, how have the links between the pairs altered by the end?
    (b) Why does the younger brother enjoy Mr Slater's company? (pp. 39–40)
    (c) Why does the younger brother feel 'unutterably lonely' (p. 42) when Luke and Elizabeth swim off together?

(d) Mr Slater too has a strong reaction to the same event, but does he have the same feelings as the boy? (p. 42)
(e) The story might have been called 'Discoveries' rather than 'The Discovery'. What discoveries are made in the story?

4. Why has the narrator chosen to tell his story some years after the events described?

   (a) Approximately how many years do you think have passed since the events described in the story took place?
   (b) 'You'll grow up one day, too. I didn't know what he meant really then, but I do now.' (p. 43) What does the narrator know now?
   (c) Why does the narrator wish it were he rather than Luke who had swum across the pool with Elizabeth? (p. 43)

John Wain (1925—)

John Wain, born in Stoke-on-Trent in the north of England, is both a poet and a novelist and short-story writer. He was also a lecturer in English literature at Reading University from 1949—55. Wain is a prolific writer and has produced four volumes of poetry, six novels, two collections of short stories as well as works of criticism and an autobiography. His works are characterized by humour and satire which avoid becoming bitter or cynical. His stories are generally concerned with ordinary people faced with the problems and decisions that make everyday life so complex.

The story

Mr Willison always regrets the fact that he never did enough sport when he was a boy. To compensate, he plans to turn his son into a great athlete. However, there is a surprise waiting for Mr Willison.

Manhood

Swiftly free-wheeling, their breath coming easily, the man and the boy steered their bicycles down the short dip which led them from woodland into open country. Then they looked ahead and saw that the road began to climb.

'Now, Rob,' said Mr Willison, settling his plump haunches* firmly on the saddle, 'just up that rise and we'll get off and have a good rest.'

'Can't we rest now?' the boy asked. 'My legs feel all funny. As if they're turning to water.'

'Rest at the top,' said Mr Willison firmly. 'Remember what I told you? The first thing any athlete has to learn is to break the fatigue barrier.'*

'I've broken it already. I was feeling tired when we were going along the main road and I—'

'When fatigue sets in, the thing to do is to keep going until it wears off. Then you get your second wind* and your second endurance.'*

'I've already done that.'

'Up we go,' said Mr Willison, 'and at the top we'll have a good rest.' He panted slightly and stood on his pedals, causing his machine to sway from side to side in a laboured manner. Rob, falling silent, pushed doggedly* at his pedals. Slowly, the pair wavered* up the straight road to the top. Once there, Mr Willison dismounted with exaggerated steadiness, laid his bicycle carefully on its side, and spread his jacket on the ground before sinking down to rest. Rob slid hastily from the saddle and flung himself full-length on the grass.

'Don't lie there,' said his father. 'You'll catch cold.'

'I'm all right. I'm warm.'

'Come and sit on this. When you're over-heated, that's just when you're prone to—'*

'I'm all *right*, Dad. I want to lie here. My back aches.'

'Your back needs strengthening, that's why it aches. It's a pity we don't live near a river where you could get some rowing.'

49

The boy did not answer, and Mr Willison, aware that he was beginning to sound like a nagging*, over-anxious parent, allowed himself to be defeated and did not press the suggestion about Rob's coming to sit on his jacket. Instead, he waited a moment and then glanced at his watch.

'Twenty to twelve. We must be going in a minute.'

'*What?* I thought we were going to have a rest.'

'Well, we're having one, aren't we?' said Mr Willison reasonably. 'I've got my breath back, so surely you must have.'

'My back still aches. I want to lie here a bit.'

'Sorry,' said Mr Willison, getting up and moving over to his bicycle. 'We've got at least twelve miles to do and lunch is at one.'

'Dad, why did we have to come so far if we've got to get back for one o'clock? I know, let's find a telephone box and ring up Mum and tell her we—'

'Nothing doing. There's no reason why two fit* men shouldn't cycle twelve miles in an hour and ten minutes.'

'But we've already done about a million miles.'

'We've done about fourteen, by my estimation.' said Mr Willison stiffly*. 'What's the good of going for a bike ride if you don't cover a bit of distance?'

He picked up his bicycle and stood waiting. Rob, with his hand over his eyes, lay motionless on the grass. His legs looked thin and white among the rich grass.

'Come on, Rob.'

The boy showed no sign of having heard. Mr Willison got on to his bicycle and began to ride slowly away. 'Rob,' he called over his shoulder, 'I'm going.'

Rob lay like a sullen* corpse* by the roadside. He looked horribly like the victim of an accident, unmarked but dead from internal injuries. Mr Willison cycled fifty yards, then a hundred, then turned in a short, irritable circle and came back to where his son lay.

'Rob, is there something the matter or are you just being awkward?'*

The boy removed his hand and looked up into his father's face. His eyes were surprisingly mild: there was no fire of rebellion in them.

'I'm tired and my back aches. I can't go on yet.'

'Look, Rob,' said Mr Willison gently. 'I wasn't going to tell you this, because I meant it to be a surprise, but when you get home you'll find a present waiting for you.'

'What kind of present?'

'Something very special I've bought for you. The man's coming this morning to fix it up. That's one reason why I suggested a bike ride this morning. He'll have done it by now.'

'What is it?'

'Aha. It's a surprise. Come on, get on your bike and let's go home and see.'

Rob sat up, then slowly clambered to his feet. 'Isn't there a short cut home?'

'I'm afraid not. It's only twelve miles.'

Rob said nothing.

'And a lot of that's downhill,' Mr Willison added brightly. His own legs were tired and his muscles fluttered* unpleasantly. In addition, he suddenly realized he was very thirsty. Rob, still without speaking, picked up his bicycle, and they pedalled away.

'Where is he?' Mrs Willison asked, coming into the garage.

'Gone up to his room,' said Mr Willison. He doubled his fist and gave the punch-ball a thudding blow. 'Seems to have fixed it pretty firmly. You gave him the instructions, I suppose.'

'What's he doing up in his room? It's lunch-time.'

'He said he wanted to rest a bit.'

'I hope you're satisfied,' said Mrs Willison. 'A lad of thirteen, nearly fourteen years of age, just when he should have a really big appetite, and when the lunch is put on the table he's *resting*—'

'Now look. I know what I'm—'

'Lying down in his room, resting, too tired to eat because you've dragged him up hill and down dale* on one of your—'

'We did nothing that couldn't be reasonably expected of a boy of his age.'

'How do you know?' Mrs Willison demanded. 'You never did anything of that kind when you were a boy. How do you know what can be reasonably—'

'Now look,' said Mr Willison again. 'When I was a boy, it was study, study, study all the time, with the fear of unemployment and insecurity in everybody's mind. I was never even given a bicycle. I never boxed. I never rowed. I never did anything to develop my physique. It was just work, work, work, pass this exam, get that certificate. Well, I did it and now I'm qualified and in a secure job. But you know as well as I do that they let me down. Nobody encouraged me to build myself up.'*

'Well, what does it matter? You're all right—'

'Grace!' Mr Willison interrupted sharply. 'I am not all right and you know it. I am under average height, my chest is flat and I'm—'

'What nonsense. You're taller than I am and I'm—'

'No son of mine is going to grow up with the same wretched physical heritage that I—'*

'No, he'll just have heart disease through overtaxing* his strength, because you haven't got the common sense to—'

'His heart is one hundred per cent all right. Not three weeks have gone by since the doctor looked at him.'

'Well, why does he get so over-tired if he's all right? Why is he lying down now instead of coming to the table, a boy of his age?'

A slender shadow blocked part of the dazzling sun in the doorway. Looking up simultaneously, the Willisons greeted their son.

'Lunch ready, Mum? I'm hungry.'

'Ready when you are,' Grace Willison beamed. 'Just wash your hands and come to the table.'

'Look, Rob,' said Mr Willison. 'If you hit it with your left hand and then catch it on the rebound with your right, it's excellent ring* training.' He dealt the punch-ball two amateurish blows. 'That's what they call a right cross,' he said.

'I think it's fine. I'll have some fun with it,' said Rob. He watched mildly as his father peeled off the padded mittens.*

'Here, slip these on,' said Mr Willison. 'They're just training gloves. They harden your fists. Of course, we can get a pair of proper gloves later. But these are specially for use with the ball.'

'Lunch,' called Mrs Willison from the house.

'Take a punch at it,' Mr Willison urged.

'Let's go and eat.'

John Wain: Manhood 53

'Go on. One punch before you go in. I haven't seen you hit it yet.'

Rob took the gloves, put on the right-hand one, and gave the punch-ball one conscientious* blow, aiming at the exact centre. 'Now let's go in,' he said.

'Lunch!'

'All right. We're coming . . .'

'Five feet eight, Rob,' said Mr Willison, folding up the wooden ruler. 'You're taller than I am. This is a great landmark.'*

'Only *just* taller.'

'But you're growing all the time. Now all you have to do is to start growing outwards as well as upwards. We'll have you in the middle of the scrum*. The heaviest forward in the pack.'*

Rob picked up his shirt and began uncertainly poking his arms into the sleeves.

'When do they pick the team?' Mr Willison asked. 'I should have thought they'd have done it by now.'

'They have done it,' said Rob. He bent down to pick up his socks from under a chair.

'They have? And you—'

'I wasn't selected,' said the boy, looking intently at the socks as if trying to detect minute* differences in colour and weave.

Mr Willison opened his mouth, closed it again, and stood for a moment looking out of the window. Then he gently laid his hand on his son's shoulder. 'Bad luck,' he said quietly.

'I tried hard,' said Rob quickly.

'I'm sure you did.'

'I played my hardest in the trial games.'*

'It's just bad luck,' said Mr Willison. 'It could happen to anybody.'

There was silence as they both continued with their dressing. A faint smell of frying rose into the air, and they could hear Mrs Willison laying the table for breakfast.

'That's it, then, for this season,'* said Mr Willison, as if to himself.

'I forgot to tell you, though,' said Rob. 'I was selected for the boxing team.'

'You *were*? I didn't know the school had one.'

'It's new. Just formed. They had some trials for it at the end of last term. I found my punching was better than most people's because I'd been getting plenty of practice with the ball.'

Mr Willison put out a hand and felt Rob's biceps.* 'Not bad, not bad at all,' he said critically. 'But if you're going to be a boxer and represent the school, you'll need more power up there. I tell you what. We'll train together.'

'That'll be fun,' said Rob. 'I'm training at school too.'

'What weight do they put you in?'

'It isn't weight, it's age. Under fifteen. Then when you get over fifteen you get classified into weights.'

'Well,' said Mr Willison, tying his tie, 'you'll be in a good position for the under-fifteens. You've got six months to play with.* And there's no reason why you shouldn't steadily put muscle on all the time. I suppose you'll be entered as a team, for tournaments and things?'

'Yes. There's a big one at the end of next term. I'll be in that.'

Confident, joking, they went down for breakfast. 'Two eggs for Rob, Mum,' said Mr Willison. 'He's in training. He's going to be a heavyweight.'

'A heavyweight what?' Mrs Willison asked, teapot in hand.

'Boxer,' Rob smiled.

Grace Willison put down the teapot, her lips compressed, and looked from one to the other. '*Boxing?*' she repeated.

'Boxing,' Mr Willison replied calmly.

'Over my dead body,'* said Mrs Willison. 'That's one sport I'm definite that he's never going in for.'

'Too late. They've picked him for the under-fifteens. He's had trials and everything.

'Is this true, Rob?' she demanded.

'Yes,' said the boy, eating rapidly.

'Well, you can just tell them you're dropping it. Baroness Summerskill—'*

'To hell with Baroness Summerskill!' her husband shouted. 'The first time he gets a chance to do something, the first time he gets picked for a team and given a chance to show what he's made of,* and you have to bring up Baroness Summerskill.'

'But it injures their brains! All those blows on the front of the skull. I've read about it—'

'Injures their brains!' Mr Willison snorted. 'Has it injured Ingemar Johansson's* brain? Why, he's one of the acutest* business men in the world!'

'Rob,' said Mrs Willison steadily, 'when you get to school, go and see the sports master and tell him you're giving up boxing.'

'There isn't a sports master. All the masters do bits of it at different times.'

'There must be one who's in charge of the boxing. All you have to do is tell him—'

'Are you ready, Rob?' said Mr Willison. 'You'll be late for school if you don't go.'

'I'm in plenty of time, Dad. I haven't finished my breakfast.'

'Never mind, push along,* old son.* You've had your egg and bacon, that's what matters. I want to talk to your mother.'

Cramming a piece of dry toast into his mouth, the boy picked up his satchel* and wandered from the room. Husband and wife sat back, glaring hot-eyed at each other.

The quarrel began, and continued for many days. In the end it was decided that Rob should continue boxing until he had represented the school at the tournament in March of the following year, and should then give it up.

'Ninety-six, ninety-seven, ninety-eight, ninety-nine, a hundred,' Mr Willison counted. 'Right, that's it. Now go and take your shower and get into bed.'

'I don't feel tired, honestly,' Rob protested.

'Who's manager here, you or me?' Mr Willison asked bluffly.* 'I'm in charge of training and you can't say my methods don't work. Fifteen solid* weeks and you start questioning my decisions on the very night of the fight?'

'It just seems silly to go to bed when I'm not—'

'My dear Rob, please trust me. No boxer ever went into a big fight without spending an hour or two in bed, resting, just before going to his dressing-room.'

'All right. But I bet none of the others are bothering to do all this.'

'That's exactly why you're going to be better than the others. Now go and get your shower before you catch cold. Leave the skipping-rope, I'll put it away.'

After Rob had gone, Mr Willison folded the skipping-rope into a neat ball and packed it away in the case that contained the boy's gloves, silk dressing gown, lace-up boxing boots, and trunks with the school badge sewn into the correct position on the right leg. There would be no harm in a little skipping, to limber up* and conquer his nervousness while waiting to go on. Humming*, he snapped down the catches of the small leather case and went into the house.

Mrs Willison did not lift her eyes from the television set as he entered. 'All ready now, Mother,' said Mr Willison. 'He's going to rest in bed now, and go along at six o'clock. I'll go with him and wait till the doors open to be sure of a ring-side seat.' He sat down on the sofa beside his wife, and tried to put his arm round her. 'Come on, love,' he said coaxingly.* 'Don't spoil my big night.'

She turned to him and he was startled to see her eyes brimming with angry tears. 'What about my big night?' she asked, her voice harsh. 'Fourteen years ago, remember? When he came into the world.'

'Well, what about it?' Mr Willison parried,* uneasily aware that the television set was quacking* and signalling on the fringe of his attention, turning the scene from clumsy tragedy into a clumsier farce.*

'Why didn't you tell me then?' she sobbed. 'Why did you let me have a son if all you were interested in was having him punched to death by a lot of rough bullet-headed louts who—'

'Take a grip on yourself,* Grace. A punch on the nose won't hurt him.'

'You're an unnatural father,' she keened. 'I don't know how you can bear to send him into that ring to be beaten and thumped — Oh, why can't you stop him now? Keep him at home? There's no *law* that compels us to—'

'That's where you're wrong, Grace,' said Mr Willison sternly. 'There is a law. The unalterable law of nature that says that the young males of the species* indulge in manly trials of strength.

Think of all the other lads who are going into the ring tonight. D'you think their mothers are sitting about crying and kicking up a fuss?* No — they're proud to have strong, masculine sons who can stand up in the ring and take a few punches.'

'Go away, please,' said Mrs Willison, sinking back with closed eyes. 'Just go right away and don't come near me until it's all over.'

'Grace!'

'Please. Please leave me alone. I can't bear to look at you and I can't bear to hear you.'

'You're hysterical,'* said Mr Willison bitterly. Rising, he went out into the hall and called up the stairs. 'Are you in bed, Rob?'

There was a slight pause and then Rob's voice called faintly, 'Could you come up, Dad?'

'Come up? Why? Is something the matter?'

'Could you come up?'

Mr Willison ran up the stairs. 'What is it?' he panted. 'D'you want something?'

'I think I've got appendicitis,'* said Rob. He lay squinting* among the pillows, his face suddenly narrow and crafty.

'I don't believe you,' said Mr Willison shortly. 'I've supervised your training for fifteen weeks and I know you're as fit as a fiddle*. You can't possibly have anything wrong with you.'

'I've got a terrible pain in my side,' said Rob. 'Low down on the right-hand side. That's where appendicitis comes, isn't it?'

Mr Willison sat down on the bed. 'Listen, Rob,' he said. 'Don't do this to me. All I'm asking you to do is to go into the ring and have one bout.* You've been picked for the school team and everyone's depending on you.'

'I'll die if you don't get the doctor,' Rob suddenly hissed. 'Mum!' he shouted.

Mrs Willison came bounding up the stairs. 'What is it, my pet?'*

'My stomach hurts. Low down on the right-hand side.'

'Appendicitis!' She whirled* to face Mr Willison. 'That's what comes of your foolishness!'

'I don't believe it,' said Mr Willison. He went out of the bedroom and down the stairs. The television was still jabbering in the living-room, and for fifteen minutes Mr Willison forced

58 *Discovery*

himself to sit staring at the strident puppets*, glistening in metallic light, as they enacted their Lilliputian rituals*. Then he went up to the bedroom again. Mrs Willison was bathing Rob's forehead.

'His temperature's normal,' she said.

'Of course his temperature's normal,' said Mr Willison. 'He doesn't want to fight, that's all.'

'Fetch the doctor,' said a voice from under the cold flannel that swathed Rob's face.

'We will, pet, if you don't get better very soon,' said Mrs Willison, darting a murderous glance at her husband.

Mr Willison slowly went downstairs. For a moment he stood looking at the telephone, then picked it up and dialled the number of the grammar school. No one answered. He replaced the receiver, went to the foot of the stairs and called, 'What's the name of the master in charge of this tournament?'

'I don't know,' Rob called weakly.

'You told me you'd been training with Mr Granger,' Mr Willison called. 'Would he know anything about it?'

Rob did not answer, so Mr Willison looked up all the Grangers in the telephone book. There were four in the town, but only one was M.A.* 'That's him,' said Mr Willison. With lead in his heart and ice in his fingers,* he dialled the number.

Mrs Granger fetched Mr Granger. Yes, he taught at the school. He was the right man. What could he do for Mr Willison?

'It's about tonight's boxing tournament?'

'Sorry, what? The line's bad.'

'*Tonight's boxing tournament.*'

'Have you got the right person?'

'You teach my son, Rob — we've just agreed on that. Well, it's about the boxing tournament he's supposed to be taking part in tonight.'

'Where?'

'Where? At the school, of course. He's representing the under-fifteens.'

There was a pause. 'I'm not quite sure what mistake you're making, Mr Willison, but I think you've got hold of the wrong end of at least one stick.'* A hearty, defensive laugh. 'If Rob belongs to a boxing-club it's certainly news to me, but in any case it can't be anything to do with the school. We don't go in for boxing.'

'Don't go in for it?'

'We don't offer it. It's not in our curriculum.'

'Oh,' said Mr Willison. 'Oh. Thank you. I must have — well, thank you.'

'Not at all. I'm glad to answer any queries. Everything's all right, I trust?'

'Oh, yes,' said Mr Willison. 'yes, thanks. Everything's all right.'

He put down the telephone, hesitated, then turned and began slowly to climb the stairs.

Glossary

The meanings given below are those which the words and phrases have as they occur in the story.

Page
49 *plump haunches*: rather round and fat bottom.
49 *to break the fatigue barrier*: to keep going when doing hard physical exercise until you no longer feel tired.
49 *second wind*: being able to breathe more easily after a first period of breathlessness.
49 *endurance*: ability to take hardship or pain.
49 *doggedly*: stubbornly.
49 *wavered*: moved unsteadily.
49 *prone to*: likely to (here, probably, likely to catch a cold).
50 *nagging*: continually finding fault.
50 *fit*: in good physical condition.
50 *stiffly*: in a formal way.
50 *sullen*: silently unforgiving.
50 *corpse*: dead body.
50 *being awkward*: deliberately causing difficulty.
51 *fluttered*: moved in a quick, irregular way.
51 *up hill and down dale*: up and down a hilly route.
52 *build myself up*: make myself stronger.
52 *wretched physical heritage that I—*: underdeveloped body I have grown up with.
52 *overtaxing*: overworking.
52 *ring*: boxing ring; place where boxers fight.
52 *peeled off the padded mittens*: took off the training gloves (used in punch-ball practice).
53 *conscientious*: done out of a sense of duty.
53 *landmark*: an important event that marks a change.
53 *scrum*: group of forwards in a rugby game who push against each other with their heads down while a ball is thrown into the middle of them.
53 *pack*: the forwards in a rugby team.
53 *minute*: maɪnˈjuːt extremely small.
53 *trial games*: games to choose the final team.
53 *season*: period of the year when rugby is played.

54 *biceps*: arm muscles.
54 *to play with*: time to spare; more time.
54 *Over my dead body*: (*idiom.*) I absolutely refuse to accept it.
54 *Baroness Summerskill*: woman politician in the House of Lords.
54 *to show what he's made of*: to prove his ability.
55 *Ingemar Johansson*: Swedish world heavyweight champion boxer (1959—1960).
55 *acutest*: cleverest; sharpest.
55 *push along*; (*coll.*) go; leave.
55 *old son*: term of affection.
55 *satchel*: bag for carrying school books.
55 *bluffly*: in a rough but good-natured way.
55 *solid*: continuous; without a break.
56 *limber up*: do exercises to make the body relaxed.
56 *humming*: singing with closed lips.
56 *coaxingly*: in a way to make her agree with him.
56 *parried*: replied to defend himself.
56 *quacking*: making ridiculous noises.
56 *farce*: a play full of ridiculous situations.
56 *Take a grip on yourself*: control yourself.
56 *species*: human and animal groups.
57 *kicking up a fuss*: (*idiom.*) making noisy objections.
57 *hysterical*: emotionally uncontrolled.
57 *appendicitis*: common disease of the intestine, which causes a sharp pain.
57 *squinting*: looking sideways with half-shut eyes.
57 *as fit as a fiddle*: (*idiom.*) in very good health.
57 *one bout*: one fight in the boxing ring.
57 *my pet*: term of affection.
57 *whirled*: turned round quickly.
58 *strident puppets*: the people on the television were like puppets making loud sharp noises.
58 *Lilliputian rituals*: Lilliput is the land of tiny people in Jonathan Swift's 'Gulliver's Travels' (1726).
58 *M.A.*: Master of Arts. A postgraduate university degree.
58 *with lead in his heart and ice in his fingers*: (*metaphors*) feeling very depressed.

62 *Discovery*

58 *got hold of the wrong end of . . . (the) stick*: (*idiom.*) misunderstood something.

Questions

1. What does the bicycle journey tell us about the physique and physical fitness of Mr Willison and his son?

    (a) How do we know Mr Willison is rather fat? (p. 49)
    (b) How do we know Rob is rather thin? (p. 50)
    (c) What details show they are both tired? (pp. 49–51)
    (d) Note the way father and son get off their bicycles. (p. 49) Which one tries to hide his tiredness? Why?
    (e) From what we know from the first few pages is it likely that Mr Willison will turn his son into a great sportsman?

2. Why is it so important to Mr Willison that his son should be fit?

    (a) Was Mr Willison fit when he was young? (pp. 51–52)
    (b) What was Mr Willison doing when he was his son's age? (p. 52)
    (c) Consider why Mr Willison speaks in the way he does in these extracts: '"That's it, then, for this season," said Mr Willison, as if to himself.' (p. 53) 'Don't spoil my big night.' (p. 56) 'Don't do this to me.' (p. 57)

3. The personalities of father and son are different. In what ways?

    (a) Who is the more forceful?
    (b) How does Rob react when he finds he has twelve more miles cycling to do, (p. 50) and what are his reactions to the new punch ball? (pp. 52–53)
    (c) How does Mr Willison react when Mrs Willison refuses to let Rob box? (pp. 54–55)

4. Is it fair to call Rob a liar because he says he is in the boxing team?

    (a) At what point in the story does Rob tell his father that

John Wain: Manhood 63

      he is in the boxing team? (pp. 53—54)
- (b) Do you think sports mean more to Rob or to his father?
- (c) What gave Rob the idea of saying he was in the *boxing* team?

5. Why is the relationship between Mr and Mrs Willison important in the story?

    (a) Are Mr and Mrs Willison in agreement about turning their son into a sportsman? On what points do they disagree?

    (b) What are the different reactions of Mr and Mrs Willison when Rob says he is ill before the 'boxing match'? (p. 57)

    (c) After Mr Willison discovers that his son is not in the boxing team (p. 59), do you think he will forgive his son or force him to continue to do more sports? What effect do you think either of these two possibilities will have on the relationship between Mr and Mrs Willison?

*   *   *   *   *

1. In both stories fathers make discoveries about their children and have to come to terms with the changed situation. Do you think it is harder for the father in 'Manhood' or in 'The Discovery' to come to terms with the discovery?

2. What makes the discovery so difficult to adjust to in these stories?

3. Is it fair to say that if parents have problems with their children then it is their own fault

    (a) in relation to the two stories?
    (b) in your own experience?

Conflict

Roald Dahl (1916–)

Roald Dahl was born in South Wales, though his parents were Norwegian. He became a fighter pilot during the Second World War and his first book of short stories, 'Over to You' (1942), deals with the tensions of war-time flying. After this came two very successful collections of short stories, 'Someone Like You' (1953) and 'Kiss Kiss' (1959), from which this story is taken. A later collection was 'Switch Bitch' (1974), and more recently he has written a novel, 'My Uncle Oswald' (1979). Dahl is fascinated by the strange and macabre. His own kind of black humour is unique as he uncovers the abnormalities that lie beneath the surface of the most conventional relationship, such as that between a man and his wife.

The story

'The Way Up to Heaven' is a story of hidden conflict in a respectable middle-class marriage. It traces the growth of this conflict and the course of events that enabled the wife to solve her problem, events which reveal an unexpected new side to her character.

The Way Up To Heaven

All her life, Mrs Foster had had an almost pathological* fear of missing a train, a plane, a boat, or even a theatre curtain. In other respects, she was not a particularly nervous woman, but the mere thought of being late on occasions like these would throw her into such a state of nerves that she would begin to twitch.* It was nothing much — just a tiny vellicating muscle in the corner of the left eye, like a secret wink — but the annoying thing was that it refused to disappear until an hour or so after the train or plane or whatever it was had been safely caught.

It was really extraordinary how in certain people a simple apprehension* about a thing like catching a train can grow into a serious obsession. At least half an hour before it was time to leave the house for the station, Mrs Foster would step out of the elevator* all ready to go, with hat and coat and gloves, and then, being quite unable to sit down, she would flutter and fidget* about from room to room until her husband, who must have been well aware of her state, finally emerged from his privacy and suggested in a cool dry voice that perhaps they had better be going now, had they not?

Mr Foster may possibly have had a right to be irritated by this foolishness of his wife's, but he could have had no excuse for increasing her misery by keeping her waiting unnecessarily. Mind you, it is by no means certain that this is what he did, yet whenever they were to go somewhere, his timing was so accurate — just a minute or two late, you understand — and his manner so bland* that it was hard to believe he wasn't purposely inflicting a nasty private little torture* of his own on the unhappy lady. And one thing he must have known — that she would never dare to call out and tell him to hurry. He had disciplined her too well for that. He must also have known that if he was prepared to wait even beyond the last moment of safety, he could drive her nearly into hysterics.* On one or two special occasions in the later years of their married life, it seemed almost as though he had *wanted* to miss the train simply in order to intensify the poor woman's suffering.

Assuming (though one cannot be sure) that the husband was guilty, what made his attitude doubly unreasonable was the fact that, with the exception of this one small irrepressible foible,* Mrs Foster was and always had been a good and loving wife. For over thirty years, she had served him loyally and well. There was no doubt about this. Even she, a very modest woman, was aware of it, and although she had for years refused to let herself believe that Mr Foster would ever consciously torment her, there had been times recently when she had caught herself beginning to wonder.

Mr Eugene Foster, who was nearly seventy years old, lived with his wife in a large six-storey house in New York City, on East Sixty-second Street, and they had four servants. It was a gloomy* place, and few people came to visit them. But on this particular morning in January, the house had come alive and there was a great deal of bustling* about. One maid was distributing bundles of dust sheets to every room, while another was draping them over the furniture. The butler was bringing down suitcases and putting them in the hall. The cook kept popping up from the kitchen to have a word with the butler, and Mrs Foster herself, in an old-fashioned fur coat and with a black hat on the top of her head, was flying from room to room and pretending to supervise these operations. Actually, she was thinking of nothing at all except that she was going to miss her plane if her husband didn't come out of his study soon and get ready.

'What time is it, Walker?' she said to the butler as she passed him.

'It's ten minutes past nine, Madam.'

'And has the car come?'

'Yes, Madam, it's waiting. I'm just going to put the luggage in now.'

'It takes an hour to get to Idlewild,'* she said. 'My plane leaves at eleven. I have to be there half an hour beforehand for the formalities.* I shall be late. I just *know* I'm going to be late.'

'I think you have plenty of time, Madam,' the butler said kindly. 'I warned Mr Foster that you must leave at nine-fifteen. There's still another five minutes.'

'Yes, Walker, I know, I know. But get the luggage in quickly, will you please?'

She began walking up and down the hall, and whenever the butler came by, she asked him the time. This, she kept telling herself, was the *one* plane she must not miss. It had taken months to persuade her husband to allow her to go. If she missed it, he might easily decide that she should cancel the whole thing. And the trouble was that he insisted on coming to the airport to see her off.

'Dear God,' she said aloud, 'I'm going to miss it. I know, I know, I *know* I'm going to miss it.' The little muscle beside the left eye was twitching madly now. The eyes themselves were very close to tears.

'What time is it, Walker?'

'It's eighteen minutes past, Madam.'

'Now I really *will* miss it!' she cried. 'Oh, I wish he would come!'

This was an important journey for Mrs Foster. She was going all alone to Paris to visit her daughter, her only child, who was married to a Frenchman. Mrs Foster didn't care much for the Frenchman, but she was fond of her daughter, and, more than that, she had developed a great yearning* to set eyes on her three grandchildren. She knew them only from the many photographs that she had received and that she kept putting up all over the house. They were beautiful, these children. She doted on them, and each time a new picture arrived she would carry it away and sit with it for a long time, staring at it lovingly and searching the small faces for signs of that old satisfying blood likeness* that meant so much. And now, lately, she had come more and more to feel that she did not really wish to live out her days in a place where she could not be near these children, and have them visit her, and take them out for walks, and buy them presents, and watch them grow. She knew, of course, that it was wrong and in a way disloyal to have thoughts like these while her husband was still alive. She knew also that although he was no longer active in his many enterprises, he would never consent to leave New York and live in Paris. It was a miracle that he had ever agreed to let her fly over there alone for six weeks to visit them. But, oh, how she wished she could live there always, and be close to them!

'Walker, what time is it?'

'Twenty-two minutes past, Madam.'

As he spoke, a door opened and Mr Foster came into the hall. He stood for a moment, looking intently at his wife, and she looked back at him — at this diminutive* but still quite dapper* old man with the huge bearded face that bore such an astonishing resemblance to those old photographs of Andrew Carnegie.*

'Well,' he said, 'I suppose perhaps we'd better get going fairly soon if you want to catch that plane.'

'*Yes*, dear — *yes!* Everything's ready. The car's waiting.'

'That's good,' he said. With his head over to one side, he was watching her closely. He had a peculiar way of cocking the head and then moving it in a series of small, rapid jerks. Because of this and because he was clasping his hands up high in front of him, near the chest, he was somehow like a squirrel standing there — a quick clever old squirrel from the Park.

'Here's Walker with your coat, dear. Put it on.'

'I'll be with you in a moment,' he said. 'I'm just going to wash my hands.'

She waited for him, and the tall butler stood beside her, holding the coat and the hat.

'Walker, will I miss it?'

'No, Madam,' the butler said. 'I think you'll make it all right.'

Then Mr Foster appeared again, and the butler helped him on with his coat. Mrs Foster hurried outside and got into the hired Cadillac. Her husband came after her, but he walked down the steps of the house slowly, pausing halfway to observe the sky and to sniff the cold morning air.

'It looks a bit foggy,' he said as he sat down beside her in the car. 'And it's always worse out there at the airport. I shouldn't be surprised if the flight's cancelled already.'

'Don't say that, dear — *please*.'

They didn't speak again until the car had crossed over the river to Long Island.*

'I arranged everything with the servants,' Mr Foster said. 'They're all going off today. I gave them half-pay for six weeks and told Walker I'd send him a telegram when we wanted them back.'

'Yes,' she said. 'He told me.'

'I'll move into the club tonight. It'll be a nice change staying at the club.'

'Yes, dear. I'll write to you.'

'I'll call in at the house occasionally to see that everything's all right and to pick up the mail.'

'But don't you really think Walker should stay there all the time to look after things?' she asked meekly.

'Nonsense. It's quite unnecessary. And anyway, I'd have to pay him full wages.'

'Oh yes,' she said. 'Of course.'

'What's more, you never know what people get up to when they're left alone in a house,' Mr Foster announced, and with that he took out a cigar and, after snipping off the end with a silver cutter, lit it with a gold lighter.

She sat still in the car with her hands clasped together tight under the rug.

'Will you write to me?' she asked.

'I'll see,' he said. 'But I doubt it. You know I don't hold with letter-writing unless there's something specific to say.'

'Yes, dear, I know. So don't you bother.'

They drove on, along Queen's Boulevard, and as they approached the flat marshland on which Idlewild is built, the fog began to thicken and the car had to slow down.

'Oh dear!' cried Mrs Foster. 'I'm *sure* I'm going to miss it now! What time is it?'

'Stop fussing,' the old man said. 'It doesn't matter anyway. It's bound to be cancelled now. They never fly in this sort of weather. I don't know why you bothered to come out.'

She couldn't be sure, but it seemed to her that there was suddenly a new note in his voice, and she turned to look at him. It was difficult to observe any change in his expression under all that hair. The mouth was what counted. She wished, as she had so often before, that she could see the mouth clearly. The eyes never showed anything except when he was in a rage.

'Of course,' he went on, 'if by any chance it *does* go, then I agree with you — you'll be certain to miss it now. Why don't you resign yourself to* that?'

She turned away and peered through the window at the fog.

It seemed to be getting thicker as they went along, and now she could only just make out the edge of the road and the margin of grassland beyond it. She knew that her husband was still looking at her. She glanced at him again, and this time she noticed with a kind of horror that he was staring intently at the little place in the corner of her left eye where she could feel the muscle twitching.

'Won't you?' he said.

'Won't I what?'

'Be sure to miss it now if it goes. We can't drive fast in this muck.'

He didn't speak to her any more after that. The car crawled on and on. The driver had a yellow lamp directed on to the edge of the road, and this helped him to keep going. Other lights, some white and some yellow, kept coming out of the fog towards them, and there was an especially bright one that followed close behind them all the time.

Suddenly, the driver stopped the car.

'There!' Mr Foster cried. 'We're stuck. I knew it.'

'No, sir,' the driver said, turning round. 'We made it. This is the airport.'

Without a word, Mrs Foster jumped out and hurried through the main entrance into the building. There was a mass of people inside, mostly disconsolate* passengers standing around the ticket counters. She pushed her way through and spoke to the clerk.

'Yes,' he said. 'Your flight is temporarily postponed. But please don't go away. We're expecting the weather to clear any moment.'

She went back to her husband who was still sitting in the car and told him the news. 'But don't you wait, dear,' she said. 'There's no sense in that.'

'I won't,' he answered. 'So long as the driver can get me back. Can you get me back, driver?'

'I think so,' the man said.

'Is the luggage out?'

'Yes, sir.'

'Good-bye, dear,' Mrs Foster said, leaning into the car and giving her husband a small kiss on the coarse grey fur of his cheek.

'Good-bye,' he answered. 'Have a good trip.'

The car drove off, and Mrs Foster was left alone.

The rest of the day was a sort of nightmare* for her. She sat for hour after hour on a bench, as close to the airline counter as possible, and every thirty minutes or so she would get up and ask the clerk if the situation had changed. She always received the same reply — that she must continue to wait, because the fog might blow away at any moment. It wasn't until after six in the evening that the loudspeakers finally announced that the flight had been postponed until eleven o'clock the next morning.

Mrs Foster didn't quite know what to do when she heard this news. She stayed sitting on her bench for at least another half-hour, wondering, in a tired, hazy* sort of way, where she might go to spend the night. She hated to leave the airport. She didn't wish to see her husband. She was terrified that in one way or another he would eventually manage to prevent her from getting to France. She would have liked to remain just where she was, sitting on the bench the whole night through. That would be the safest. But she was already exhausted, and it didn't take her long to realize that this was a ridiculous thing for an elderly lady to do. So in the end she went to a phone and called the house.

Her husband, who was on the point of leaving for the club, answered it himself. She told him the news, and asked whether the servants were still there.

'They've all gone,' he said.

'In that case, dear, I'll just get myself a room somewhere for the night. And don't you bother yourself about it at all.'

'That would be foolish,' he said. 'You've got a large house here at your disposal. Use it.'

'But, dear, it's *empty*.'

'Then I'll stay with you myself.'

'There's no food in the house. There's nothing.'

'Then eat before you come in. Don't be so stupid, woman. Everything you do, you seem to want to make a fuss about it.'

'Yes,' she said. 'I'm sorry. I'll get myself a sandwich here, and then I'll come on in.'

Outside, the fog had cleared a little, but it was still a long, slow drive in the taxi, and she didn't arrive back at the house on Sixty-second Street until fairly late.

Her husband emerged from his study when he heard her coming in. 'Well,' he said, standing by the study door, 'how was Paris?'

'We leave at eleven in the morning,' she answered. 'It's definite.'

'You mean if the fog clears.'

'It's clearing now. There's a wind coming up.'

'You look tired,' he said. 'You must have had an anxious day.'

'It wasn't very comfortable. I think I'll go straight to bed.'

'I've ordered a car for the morning.' he said. 'Nine o'clock.'

'Oh, thank you, dear. And I certainly hope you're not going to bother to come all the way to see me off.'

'No,' he said slowly. 'I don't think I will. But there's no reason why you shouldn't drop me at the club on your way.'

She looked at him, and at that moment he seemed to be standing a long way off from her, beyond some borderline. He was suddenly so small and far away that she couldn't be sure what he was doing, or what he was thinking, or even what he was.

'The club is downtown,' she said. 'It isn't on the way to the airport.'

'But you'll have plenty of time, my dear. Don't you want to drop me at the club?'

'Oh, yes — of course.'

'That's good. Then I'll see you in the morning at nine.'

She went up to her bedroom on the second floor, and she was so exhausted from her day that she fell asleep soon after she lay down.

Next morning, Mrs Foster was up early, and by eight-thirty she was downstairs and ready to leave.

Shortly after nine, her husband appeared. 'Did you make any coffee?' he asked.

'No, dear. I thought you'd get a nice breakfast at the club. The car is here. It's been waiting. I'm all ready to go.'

They were standing in the hall — they always seemed to be meeting in the hall nowadays — she with her hat and coat and purse, he in a curiously cut Edwardian jacket with high lapels.

'Your luggage?'

'It's at the airport.'

Roald Dahl: The Way Up To Heaven 75

'Ah yes,' he said. 'Of course. And if you're going to take me to the club first, I suppose we'd better get going fairly soon, hadn't we?'

'Yes!' she cried. 'Oh, yes – *please*!'

'I'm just going to get a few cigars. I'll be right with you. You get in the car.'

She turned and went out to where the chauffeur was standing, and he opened the car door for her as she approached.

'What time is it?' she asked him.

'About nine-fifteen.'

Mr Foster came out five minutes later, and watching him as he walked slowly down the steps, she noticed that his legs were like goat's legs in those narrow stovepipe trousers that he wore. As on the day before, he paused half-way down to sniff the air and to examine the sky. The weather was still not quite clear, but there was a wisp of sun coming through the mist.

'Perhaps you'll be lucky this time,' he said as he settled himself beside her in the car.

'Hurry, please,' she said to the chauffer. 'Don't bother about the rug. I'll arrange the rug. Please get going. I'm late.'

The man went back to his seat behind the wheel and started the engine.

'*Just* a moment!' Mr Foster said suddenly. 'Hold it a moment, chauffeur, will you?'

'What is it, dear?' She saw him searching the pockets of his overcoat.

'I had a little present I wanted you to take to Ellen,' he said. 'Now, where on earth is it? I'm sure I had it in my hand as I came down.'

'I never saw you carrying anything. What sort of present?'

'A little box wrapped up in white paper. I forgot to give it to you yesterday. I don't want to forget it today.'

'A little box!' Mrs Foster cried. 'I never saw any little box!' She began hunting frantically in the back of the car.

Her husband continued searching through the pockets of his coat. Then he unbuttoned the coat and felt around in his jacket. 'Confound it,'* he said, 'I must've left it in my bedroom. I won't be a moment.'

'Oh, *please*!' she cried. 'We haven't got time! *Please* leave it! You can mail it.* It's only one of those silly combs anyway. You're always giving her combs.'

'And what's wrong with combs, may I ask?' he said, furious that she should have forgotten herself for once.

'Nothing, dear, I'm sure. But . . .'

'Stay here!' he commanded. 'I'm going to get it.'

'Be quick, dear! Oh, *please* be quick!'

She sat still, waiting and waiting.

'Chauffeur, what time is it?'

The man had a wristwatch, which he consulted. 'I make it nearly nine-thirty.'

'Can we get to the airport in an hour?'

'Just about.'

At this point, Mrs Foster suddenly spotted a corner of something white wedged down in the crack of the seat on the side where her husband had been sitting. She reached over and pulled out a small paper-wrapped box, and at the same time she couldn't help noticing that it was wedged down firm and deep, as though with the help of a pushing hand.

'Here it is!' she cried. 'I've found it! Oh dear, and now he'll be up there for ever searching for it! Chauffeur, quickly — run in and call him down, will you please?'

The chauffeur, a man with a small rebellious Irish mouth, didn't care very much for any of this, but he climbed out of the car and went up the steps to the front door of the house. Then he turned and came back. 'Door's locked,' he announced. 'You got a key?'

'Yes — wait a minute.' She began hunting madly in her purse. The little face was screwed up tight with anxiety, the lips pushed outward like a spout.*

'Here it is! No — I'll go myself. It'll be quicker. I know where he'll be.'

She hurried out of the car and up the steps to the front door, holding the key in one hand. She slid the key into the keyhole and was about to turn it — and then she stopped. Her head came up, and she stood there absolutely motionless, her whole body arrested* right in the middle of all this hurry to turn the key and get into the house, and she waited — five, six, seven, eight, nine, ten seconds, she waited. The way she was standing there, with her head in the air and the body so tense, it seemed as though she were listening for the repetition of some sound that she had heard a moment before from a place far away inside the house.

Yes — quite obviously she was listening. Her whole attitude was a *listening* one. She appeared actually to be moving one of her ears closer and closer to the door. Now it was right up against the door, and for still another few seconds she remained in that position, head up, ear to door, hand on key, about to enter but not entering, trying instead, or so it seemed, to hear and to analyse* these sounds that were coming faintly from this place deep within the house.

Then, all at once, she sprang to life again. She withdrew the key from the door and came running back down the steps.

'It's too late!' she cried to the chauffeur. 'I can't wait for him, I simply can't. I'll miss the plane. Hurry now, driver, hurry! To the airport!'

The chauffeur, had he been watching her closely, might have noticed that her face had turned absolutely white and that the whole expression had suddenly altered. There was no longer that rather soft and silly look. A peculiar hardness had settled itself upon the features. The little mouth, usually so flabby,* was now tight and thin, the eyes were bright, and the voice, when she spoke, carried a new note of authority.

'Hurry, driver, hurry!'

'Isn't your husband travelling with you?' the man asked, astonished.

'Certainly not! I was only going to drop him at the club. It won't matter. He'll understand. He'll get a cab. Don't sit there talking, man. *Get going!* I've got a plane to catch for Paris!'

With Mrs Foster urging him from the back seat, the man drove fast all the way, and she caught her plane with a few minutes to spare. Soon she was high up over the Atlantic, reclining comfortably in her aeroplane chair, listening to the hum of the motors, heading for Paris at last. The new mood was still with her. She felt remarkably strong and, in a queer sort of way, wonderful. She was a trifle* breathless with it all, but this was more from pure astonishment at what she had done than anything else, and as the plane flew farther and farther away from New York and East Sixty-second Street, a great sense of calmness began to settle upon her. By the time she reached Paris, she was just as strong and cool and calm as she could wish.

She met her grandchildren, and they were even more beautiful in the flesh than in their photographs. They were like angels, she told herself, so beautiful they were. And every day she took them for walks, and fed them cakes, and bought them presents, and told them charming stories.

Once a week, on Tuesdays, she wrote a letter to her husband — a nice, chatty letter — full of news and gossip, which always ended with the words 'Now be sure to take your meals regularly, dear, although this is something I'm afraid you may not be doing when I'm not with you.'

When the six weeks were up, everybody was sad that she had to return to America, to her husband. Everybody, that is, except her. Surprisingly, she didn't seem to mind as much as one might have expected, and when she kissed them all good-bye, there was something in her manner and in the things she said that appeared to hint at the possibility of a return in the not too distant future.

However, like the faithful wife she was, she did not overstay her time. Exactly six weeks after she had arrived, she sent a cable* to her husband and caught the plane back to New York.

Arriving at Idlewild, Mrs Foster was interested to observe that there was no car to meet her. It is possible that she might even have been a little amused. But she was extremely calm and did not overtip* the porter who helped her into a taxi with her baggage.

New York was colder than Paris, and there were lumps of dirty snow lying in the gutters of the streets. The taxi drew up before the house on Sixty-second Street, and Mrs Foster persuaded the driver to carry her two large cases to the top of the steps. Then she paid him off and rang the bell. She waited, but there was no answer. Just to make sure, she rang again, and she could hear it tinkling shrilly* far away in the pantry,* at the back of the house. But still no one came.

So she took out her own key and opened the door herself.

The first thing she saw as she entered was a great pile of mail lying on the floor where it had fallen after being slipped through the letter box. The place was dark and cold. A dust sheet was still draped over the grandfather clock. In spite of the cold, the atmosphere was peculiarly oppressive,* and there was a faint and curious odour in the air that she had never smelled before.

She walked quickly across the hall and disappeared for a moment around the corner to the left, at the back. There was something deliberate and purposeful about this action; she had the air of a woman who is off to investigate a rumour or to confirm a suspicion. And when she returned a few seconds later, there was a little glimmer of satisfaction on her face.

She paused in the centre of the hall, as though wondering what to do next. Then, suddenly, she turned and went across into her husband's study. On the desk she found his address book, and after hunting through it for a while she picked up the phone and dialled a number.

'Hello,' she said. 'Listen — this is Nine East Sixty-second Street. . . . Yes, that's right. Could you send someone round as soon as possible, do you think? Yes, it seems to be stuck between the second and third floors. At least, that's where the indicator's pointing. . . . Right away? Oh, that's very kind of you. You see, my legs aren't any too good for walking up a lot of stairs. Thank you so much. Good-bye.'

She replaced the receiver and sat there at her husband's desk, patiently waiting for the man who would be coming soon to repair the lift.

80 Conflict

Glossary

The meanings given below are those which the words and phrases have as they occur in the story.

Page
67 *pathological*: like a disease.
67 *twitch*: have a sudden, uncontrollable muscle movement.
67 *apprehension*: feeling of uneasiness or anxiety.
67 *elevator*: (A.E.) lift.
67 *flutter and fidget*: move about in a nervous, irregular way.
67 *bland*: smooth.
67 *torture*: action deliberately causing pain.
67 *hysterics*: uncontrollable outburst of emotion.
68 *irrepressible foible*: personal peculiarity which she couldn't control.
68 *gloomy*: dark and cheerless.
68 *bustling*: busy moving.
68 *Idlewild*: airport outside New York City; now Kennedy Airport.
68 *formalities*: official checks at the airport.
69 *great yearning*: strong desire.
69 *blood likeness*: family similarity.
70 *diminutive*: tiny.
70 *dapper*: neat in appearance.
70 *Andrew Carnegie*: 19th century American industrialist.
70 *Long Island*: the large island east of New York.
71 *resign yourself to*: accept without complaining.
72 *disconsolate*: unhappy; disappointed.
73 *nightmare*: bad, frightening dream.
73 *hazy*: unclear.
75 *Confound it*: an expression of annoyance.
76 *mail it*: (A.E.) send it by post.
76 *spout*: open end of a pipe through which liquid pours, as on a tea pot.
76 *arrested*: stopped.
77 *analyse*: work out the meaning of.
77 *flabby*: loose and fleshy.
77 *a trifle*: slightly; a little.
78 *cable*: (A.E.) telegram.

Roald Dahl: The Way Up To Heaven 81

78 *overtip*: give too much extra money to.
78 *shrilly*: in a sharp, high way.
78 *pantry*: room near the kitchen of a large house in which articles for the table are kept.
79 *oppressive*: heavy and uncomfortable.

Questions

1. Is the Fosters' marriage happy and trouble-free?

    (a) Does Mrs Foster have a habit which is a problem and causes her unhappiness? (p. 67)
    (b) Is Mr Foster sympathetic to her and does he do all he can to make things easier for her? (p. 67)
    (c) Has Mrs Foster always been a good wife? (p. 68)
    (d) Does she realize Mr Foster's real intentions on occasions when he keeps her waiting? (p. 68)

2. What evidence is there of Mr Foster's attitude to his wife?

    (a) When Mrs Foster is in a hurry to leave for the airport the first time, does Mr Foster also hurry to join her in the car? (pp. 69–70)
    (b) Does Mr Foster feel unhappy about having to stay in the club while his wife is away and will he answer her letters? (p. 71)
    (c) What does he stare at while they are in the car? (p. 72)
    (d) Does he stay with her at the airport or show affection and sorrow because she is going away? (p. 72)
    (e) What are his first words when she returns from the airport? (p. 74)
    (f) The next morning, is Mr Foster ready to leave at the arranged time and why does he say he has left the white parcel in the house? (p. 75)

3. How do Mrs Foster's feelings about her husband develop?

    (a) What does she begin to suspect about his actions? (p. 68)
    (b) Does she feel close to her husband when she returns from the airport for the night? (p. 74)

82 Conflict

  (c) 'They always seemed to be meeting in the hall nowadays.' (p. 74) What does this tell us about their relationship?

4. How does Mrs Foster change from the time when she goes back to the house to speak to her husband? (p. 76)

   (a) Why does she stop?
   (b) What is she listening to?
   (c) How do her manner and appearance change when she decides to go to the airport immediately? (p. 77)
   (d) What is the new mood which develops while she is on the plane? (pp. 77-78)

5. How does Mrs Foster feel and act when she returns from France?

   (a) Is she unwilling to come back? (p. 78)
   (b) Is she surprised when she finds that there is no car to collect her at the airport? (p. 78)
   (c) What does she find when she opens the front door and what does she smell? (p. 79)
   (d) What does she do when she gets inside the house and what kind of expression does she have on her face? (p. 79)
   (e) What has happened to the elevator?
   (f) What has happened to Mr Foster?

6. What does Mrs Foster say in the letters she wrote from Paris? (p. 78). In what way are the letters very ironic?

7. Which of the following remarks do you agree with, and which do you disagree with and why?

   (a) Mrs Foster's decision at the front door is one you can understand and sympathize with.
   (b) Mr Foster deserved what he got.
   (c) Mrs Foster should have separated from her husband a long time before the time of the story.
   (d) Mrs Foster deserves to live happily with her grandchildren in France.

(e) Mrs Foster murdered her husband.
(f) Mrs Foster simply took full advantage of an unfortunate accident.
(g) It is very surprising that Mrs Foster didn't feel guilty about her actions.

John Steinbeck (1902–68)

John Steinbeck was a native of California, U.S.A., and many of his stories concern the lives of those, originally from many different cultures, who settled there, often as farmers and ranchers. He is among the best-known American writers of this century and was awarded the Nobel Prize for Literature in 1962. His novels include 'Tortilla Flat' (1935), 'Of Mice and Men' (1937), 'The Grapes of Wrath' (1939) and 'East of Eden' (1952). 'The Murder' comes from the collection of short stories 'The Long Valley', originally published in 1938.

The story

'The Murder' is set in the early days of settlement in California. It is the story of a marriage between people of different nationalities, of the violent climax to the growing problem between them and of the surprising outcome.

The Murder

This happened a number of years ago in Monterey County, in central California. The Cañon del Castillo is one of those valleys in the Santa Lucia range* which lie between its many spurs and ridges.* From the main Cañon del Castillo a number of little arroyos* cut back into the mountains, oak-wooded canyons,* heavily brushed with poison oak and sage. At the head of the canyon there stands a tremendous stone castle, buttressed* and towered like those strongholds the Crusaders* put up in the path of their conquests. Only a close visit to the castle shows it to be a strange accident of time and water and erosion working on soft, stratified sandstone.* In the distance the ruined battlements, the gates, the towers, even the arrow slits, require little imagination to make out.

Below the castle, on the nearly level floor of the canyon, stand the old ranch* house, a weathered and mossy barn and a warped* feeding-shed for cattle. The house is deserted; the doors, swinging on rusted hinges, squeal and bang on nights when the wind courses down from the castle. Not many people visit the house. Sometimes a crowd of boys tramp through the rooms, peering into empty closets and loudly defying* the ghosts they deny.

Jim Moore, who owns the land, does not like to have people about the house. He rides up from his new house, farther down the valley, and chases the boys away. He has put 'No Trespassing'* signs on his fences to keep curious and morbid* people out. Sometimes he thinks of burning the old house down, but then a strange and powerful relation with the swinging doors, the blind and desolate windows, forbids* the destruction. If he should burn the house he would destroy a great and important piece of his life. He knows that when he goes to town with his plump* and still pretty wife, people turn and look at his retreating back with awe* and some admiration.

86 Conflict

Jim Moore was born in the old house and grew up in it. He knew every grained and weathered board of the barn, every smooth, worn manger-rack.* His mother and father were both dead when he was thirty. He celebrated his majority* by raising a beard. He sold the pigs and decided never to have any more. At last he bought a fine Guernsey bull to improve his stock, and he began to go to Monterey on Saturday nights, to get drunk and to talk with the noisy girls of the Three Star.

Within a year Jim Moore married Jelka Sepic, a Jugo-Slav girl, daughter of a heavy and patient farmer of Pine Canyon. Jim was not proud of her foreign family, of her many brothers and sisters and cousins, but he delighted in her beauty. Jelka had eyes as large and questioning as a doe's* eyes. Her nose was thin and sharply faceted, and her lips were deep and soft. Jelka's skin always startled* Jim, for between night and night he forgot how beautiful it was. She was so smooth and quiet and gentle, such a good housekeeper, that Jim often thought with disgust of her father's advice on the wedding day. The old man, bleary and bloated* with festival beer, elbowed Jim in the ribs and grinned suggestively,* so that his little dark eyes almost disappeared behind puffed and wrinkled lids.

'Don't be big fool, now,' he said. 'Jelka is Slav girl. He's* not like American girl. If he is bad, beat him. If he's good too long, beat him too. I beat his mama. Papa beat my mama. Slav girl! He's not like a man* that don't beat hell out of him.'

'I wouldn't beat Jelka,' Jim said.

The father giggled and nudged him again with his elbow, 'Don't be big fool,' he warned. 'Sometime you see.' He rolled back to the beer barrel.

Jim found soon enough that Jelka was not like American girls. She was very quiet. She never spoke first, but only answered his questions, and then with soft short replies. She learned her husband as she learned passages of Scripture.* After they had been married a while, Jim never wanted for any habitual thing* in the house but Jelka had it ready for him before he could ask. She was a fine wife, but there was no companionship in her. She never talked. Her great eyes followed him, and when he smiled, sometimes she smiled too, a distant and covered* smile. Her knitting and mending and sewing were interminable.* There she sat, watching her wise hands, and she seemed to regard with wonder and pride the little white hands that could do such nice and useful things. She was so much like an animal that sometimes Jim patted her head and neck under the same impulse that made him stroke a horse.

In the house Jelka was remarkable. No matter what time Jim came in from the hot dry range* or from the bottom farm land, his dinner was exactly, steaming ready for him. She watched while he ate, and pushed the dishes close when he needed them, and filled his cup when it was empty.

Early in the marriage he told her things that happened on the farm, but she smiled at him as a foreigner does who wishes to be agreeable even though he doesn't understand.

'The stallion cut himself on the barbed wire,' he said.

And she replied 'Yes,' with a downward inflection that had neither question nor interest.

He realized before long that he could not get in touch* with her in any way. If she had a life apart,* it was so remote as to be beyond his reach. The barrier in her eyes was not one that could be removed, for it was neither hostile nor intentional.

At night he stroked her straight black hair and her unbelievably smooth golden shoulders, and she whimpered* a little with pleasure. Only in the climax of his embrace did she seem to have a life apart, fierce and passionate. And then immediately she lapsed into* the alert and painfully dutiful wife.

'Why don't you ever talk to me?' he demanded. 'Don't you want to talk to me?'

'Yes,' she said. 'What do you want me to say?' She spoke the language of his race out of a mind that was foreign to his race.

When a year had passed, Jim began to crave* the company of women, the chattery exchange of small talk, the shrill pleasant insults, the shame-sharpened vulgarity.* He began to go again to town, to drink and to play with the noisy girls of the Three Star. They liked him there for his firm, controlled face and for his readiness to laugh.

'Where's your wife?' they demanded.

'Home in the barn,' he responded. It was a never-failing joke.

88 *Conflict*

Saturday afternoons he saddled a horse and put a rifle in the scabbard in case he should see a deer. Always he asked: 'You don't mind staying alone?'

'No I don't mind.'

At once he asked: 'Suppose someone should come?'

Her eyes sharpened for a moment, and then she smiled. 'I would send them away,' she said.

'I'll be back about noon tomorrow. It's too far to ride in the night.' He felt that she knew where he was going, but she never protested nor gave any sign of disapproval. 'You should have a baby,' he said.

Her face lighted up. 'Some time God will be good,' she said eagerly.

He was sorry for her loneliness. If only she visited with the other women of the canyon she would be less lonely, but she had no gift for visiting. Once every month or so she put horses to the buckboard* and went to spend an afternoon with her mother, and with the brood of brothers and sisters and cousins who lived in her father's house.

'A fine time you'll have,' Jim said to her. 'You'll gabble your crazy language like ducks for a whole afternoon. You'll giggle* with that big grown cousin of yours with the embarrassed face. If I could find any fault with you, I'd call you a damn foreigner.' He remembered how she blessed the bread with the sign of the cross before she put it in the oven, how she knelt at the bedside every night, how she had a holy picture tacked* to the wall in the closet.

One Saturday in a hot dusty June, Jim cut oats in the farm flat*. The day was long. It was after six o'clock when the mower tumbled the last band* of oats. He drove the clanking machine up into the barnyard and backed it into the implement shed, and there he unhitched the horses and turned them out to graze on the hills over Sunday. When he entered the kitchen Jelka was just putting his dinner on the table. He washed his hands and face and sat down to eat.

'I'm tired,' he said, 'but I think I'll go to Monterey anyway. There'll be a full moon.'

Her soft eyes smiled.

'I'll tell you what I'll do,' he said. 'If you would like to go, I'll hitch up a rig* and take you with me.'

She smiled again and shook her head. 'No, the stores would be closed. I would rather stay here.'

'Well, all right, I'll saddle the horse then. I didn't think I was going. The stock's all turned out. Maybe I can catch a horse easy. Sure you don't want to go?'

'If it was early, and I could go to the stores — but it will be ten o'clock when you get there.'

'Oh, no — well, anyway, on horseback I'll make it a little after nine.'

Her mouth smiled to itself, but her eyes watched him for the development of a wish. Perhaps because he was tired from the long day's work, he demanded: 'What are you thinking about?'

'Thinking about? I remember, you used to ask that nearly every day when we were first married.'

'But what are you?' he insisted irritably.

'Oh — I'm thinking about the eggs under the black hen.' She got up and went to the big calendar on the wall. 'They will hatch tomorrow or maybe Monday.'

It was almost dusk* when he had finished shaving and putting on his blue serge suit and his new boots. Jelka had the dishes washed and put away. As Jim went through the kitchen he saw that she had taken the lamp to the table near the window, and that she sat beside it knitting a brown wool sock.

'Why do you sit there tonight?' he asked. 'You always sit over here. You do funny things sometimes.'

Her eyes arose slowly from her flying hands. 'The moon,' she said quietly. 'You said it would be full tonight. I want to see the moon rise.'

'But you're silly. You can't see it from that window. I thought you knew direction better than that.'

She smiled remotely. 'I will look out of the bedroom window, then.'

Jim put on his black hat and went out. Walking through the dark empty barn, he took a halter* from the rack. On the grassy sidehill he whistled high and shrill. The horses stopped feeding and moved slowly in towards him, and stopped twenty feet away.

Carefully he approached his bay gelding* and moved his hand from its rump along its side and up and over its neck.** The halter-strap clicked in its buckle. Jim turned and led the horse back to the barn. He threw his saddle on and cinched it tight, put his silver-bound bridle over the stiff ears, buckled the throat latch, knotted the tie-rope about the gelding's neck and fastened the neat coil-end to the saddle string. Then he slipped the halter and led the horse to the house. A radiant crown of soft red light lay over the eastern hills. The full moon would rise before the valley had completely lost the daylight.

In the kitchen Jelka still knitted by the window. Jim strode to the corner of the room and took up his 30-30 carbine.* As he rammed cartridges into the magazine,* he said: 'The moon glow is on the hills. If you are going to see it rise, you better go outside now. It's going to be a good red one at rising.'

'In a moment,' she replied, 'when I come to the end here.' He went to her and patted her sleek head.

'Good night. I'll probably be back by noon tomorrow.' Her dusky black eyes followed him out of the door.

Jim thrust the rifle into his saddle-scabbard, and mounted and swung his horse down the canyon. On his right, from behind the blackening hills, the great red moon slid rapidly up. The double light of the day's last afterglow and the rising moon thickened the outlines of the trees and gave a mysterious new perspective to the hills. The dusty oaks shimmered* and glowed, and the shade under them was black as velvet. A huge, long-legged shadow of a horse and half a man rode to the left and slightly ahead of Jim. From the ranches near and distant came the sound of dogs tuning up for a night of song. And the roosters crowed,* thinking a new dawn had come too quickly. Jim lifted the gelding to a trot. The spattering hoof-steps echoed back from the castle behind him. He thought of blonde May at the Three Star at Monterey. 'I'll be late. Maybe someone else'll have her,' he thought. The moon was clear of the hills now.

Jim had gone a mile when he heard the hoofbeats of a horse coming towards him. A horseman cantered up and pulled to a stop. 'That you, Jim?'

'Yes. Oh, hello, George.'

'I was just riding up to your place. I want to tell you — you know the springboard* at the upper end of my land?'

'Yes, I know.'

'Well, I was up there this afternoon. I found a dead campfire and a calf's head and feet. The skin was in the fire, half burned, but I pulled it out and it had your brand.'*

[*foreshadowing*]

'The hell,' said Jim. 'How old was the fire?'

'The ground was still warm in the ashes. Last night, I guess. Look, Jim, I can't go up with you. I've got to go to town, but I thought I'd tell you, so you could take a look around.'

Jim asked quietly: 'Any idea how many men?'

'No. I didn't look close.'

'Well, I guess I better go up and look. I was going to town too. But if there are thieves working, I don't want to lose any more stock. I'll cut up through your land if you don't mind, George.'

'I'd go with you, but I've got to go to town. You got a gun with you?'

'Oh yes, sure. Here under my leg. Thanks for telling me.'

'That's all right. Cut through any place you want. Good night.' The neighbour turned his horse and cantered back in the direction from which he had come.

For a few moments Jim sat in the moonlight, looking down at his stilted* shadow. He pulled his rifle from its scabbard, levered a cartridge into the chamber, and held the gun across the pommel of his saddle. He turned left from the road, went up the little ridge, through the oak grove, over the grassy hogback* and down the other side into the next canyon.

In half an hour he had found the deserted camp. He turned over the heavy, leathery calf's head and felt its dusty tongue to judge by the dryness how long it had been dead. He lighted a match and looked at his brand on the half-burned hide. At last he mounted his horse again, rode over the bald grassy hills and crossed into his own land.

A warm summer wind was blowing on the hilltops. The moon, as it quartered up the sky, lost its redness and turned the colour of strong tea. Among the hills the coyotes* were singing, and the dogs at the ranch houses below joined them with broken-hearted howling. The dark green oaks below and the yellow summer grass showed their colours in the moonlight.

Jim followed the sound of the cowbells to his herd, and found them eating quietly, and a few deer feeding with them. He listened for the sound of hoofbeats* or the voices of men on the wind.

It was after eleven when he turned his horse towards home. He rounded the west tower of the sandstone castle, rode through the shadow and out into the moonlight again. Below, the roofs of his barn and house shone dully. The bedroom window cast back a streak of reflection.

The feeding horses lifted their heads as Jim came down through the pasture. Their eyes glinted redly when they turned their heads.

Jim had almost reached the corral fence — he heard a horse stamping in the barn. His hand jerked the gelding down. He listened. It came again, the stamping from the barn. Jim lifted his rifle and dismounted silently. He turned his horse loose and crept towards the barn.

In the blackness he could hear the grinding of the horse's teeth as it chewed hay. He moved along the barn until he came to the occupied stall. After a moment of listening he scratched a match on the butt of his rifle. A saddled and bridled horse was tied in the stall. The bit* was slipped under the chin and the cinch* loosened. The horse stopped eating and turned its head towards the light.

Jim blew out the match and walked quickly out of the barn. He sat on the edge of the horse-trough* and looked into the water. His thoughts came so slowly that he put them into words and said them under his breath.

'Shall I look through the window? No. My head would throw a shadow in the room.'

He regarded the rifle in his hand. Where it had been rubbed and handled, the black gun finish had worn off, leaving the metal silvery.

At last he stood up with decision and moved towards the house. At the steps, an extended foot tried each board tenderly before he put his weight on it. The three ranch dogs came out from under the house and shook themselves, stretched and sniffed, wagged their tails and went back to bed.

John Steinbeck: The Murder 93

The kitchen was dark, but Jim knew where every piece of furniture was. He put out his hand and touched the corner of the table, a chair back, the towel hanger, as he went along. He crossed the room so silently that even he could hear only his breath and the whisper of his trouserlegs together, and the beating of his watch in his pocket. The bedroom door stood open and spilled a patch of moonlight on the kitchen floor. Jim reached the door at last and peered* through.

The moonlight lay on the white bed. Jim saw Jelka lying on her back, one soft bare arm flung across her forehead and eyes. He could not see who the man was, for his head was turned away. Jim watched, holding his breath. Then Jelka twitched* in her sleep and the man rolled his head and sighed — Jelka's cousin, her grown, embarrassed cousin.

Jim turned and quickly stole back across the kitchen and down the back steps. He walked up the yard to the water-trough again, and sat down on the edge of it. The moon was white as chalk, and it swam in the water, and lighted the straws and barley dropped by the horses' mouths. Jim could see the mosquito wrigglers, tumbling up and down, end over end, in the water, and he could see a newt lying in the sun moss in the bottom of the trough.

He cried a few dry, hard, smothered sobs,* and wondered why, for his thought was of the grassed hilltops and of the lonely summer wind whisking along.

His thoughts turned to the way his mother used to hold a bucket to catch the throat blood when his father killed a pig. She stood as far away as possible and held the bucket at arms'-length to keep her clothes from getting spattered.

Jim dipped his hand into the trough and stirred the moon* to broken, swirling streams of light. He wetted his forehead with his damp hands and stood up. This time he did not move so quietly, but he crossed the kitchen on tiptoe and stood in the bedroom door. Jelka moved her arm and opened her eyes a little. Then the eyes sprang wide, then they glistened with moisture. Jim looked into her eyes; his face was empty of expression. A little drop ran out of Jelka's nose and lodged in the hollow of her upper lip. She stared back at him.

Jim cocked* the rifle. The steel click sounded through the house. The man on the bed stirred uneasily in his sleep. Jim's hands were quivering. He raised the gun to his shoulder and held it tightly to keep from shaking. Over the sights he saw the little white square between the man's brows and hair. The front sight wavered a moment and then came to rest.

The gun crash tore the air. Jim, still looking down the barrel, saw the whole bed jolt under the blow. A small, black, bloodless hole was in the man's forehead. But behind, the hollow-point took brain and bone and splashed them on the pillow.

Jelka's cousin gurgled* in his throat. His hands came crawling out from under the covers like big white spiders, and they walked for a moment, then shuddered and fell quiet.

Jim looked slowly back at Jelka. Her nose was running. Her eyes had moved from him to the end of the rifle. She whined softly, like a cold puppy.

Jim turned in panic. His boot heels beat on the kitchen floor, but outside, he moved slowly towards the water-trough again. There was a taste of salt in his throat, and his heart heaved painfully. He pulled his hat off and dipped his head into the water. Then he leaned over and vomited on the ground. In the house he could hear Jelka moving about. She whimpered like a puppy. Jim straightened up, weak and dizzy.

He walked tiredly through the corral and into the pasture. His saddled horse came at his whistle. Automatically he tightened the cinch, mounted and rode away, down the road to the valley. The squat black shadow travelled under him. The moon sailed high and white. The uneasy dogs barked monotonously.

At daybreak a buckboard and pair* trotted up to the ranch yard, scattering the chickens. A deputy sheriff* and a coroner* sat in the seat. Jim Moore half reclined against his saddle in the wagon-box. His tired gelding followed behind. The deputy sheriff set the brake and wrapped the lines around it. The men dismounted.

Jim asked: 'Do I have to go in? I'm too tired and wrought up* to see it now.'

The coroner pulled his lip and studied. 'Oh, I guess not. We'll tend to* things and look around.'

John Steinbeck: The Murder

Jim sauntered away* towards the water-trough. 'Say,' he called, 'kind of clean up a little, will you? You know.'

The men went on into the house.

In a few minutes they emerged, carrying the stiffened body between them. It was wrapped in a comforter.* They eased it up into the wagon-box. Jim walked back towards them. 'Do I have to go in with you now?'

'Where's your wife, Mr Moore?' the deputy sheriff demanded.

'I don't know,' he said wearily. 'She's somewhere around.'

'You're sure you didn't kill her too?'

'No. I didn't touch her. I'll find her and bring her in this afternoon. That is, if you don't want me to go in with you now.'

'We've got your statement,'* the coroner said. 'And by God, we've got eyes, haven't we, Will? Of course there's a technical charge of murder against you, but it'll be dismissed.* Always is in this part of the country. Go kind of light on your wife, Mr Moore.'

'I won't hurt her,' said Jim.

He stood and watched the buckboard jolt away. He kicked his feet reluctantly* in the dust. The hot June sun showed its face over the hills and flashed viciously on the bedroom window.

Jim went slowly into the house, and brought out a nine-foot, loaded bull whip. He crossed the yard and walked into the barn. And as he climbed the ladder to the hay-loft, he heard the high, puppy whimpering start.

When Jim came out of the barn again, he carried Jelka over his shoulder. By the water-trough he set her tenderly on the ground. Her hair was littered with bits of hay. The back of her shirtwaist was streaked with blood.

Jim wetted his bandana* at the pipe and washed her bitten lips, and washed her face and brushed back her hair. Her dusty black eyes followed every move he made.

'You hurt me,' she said. 'You hurt me bad.'

He nodded gravely. 'Bad as I could without killing you.'

The sun shone hotly on the ground. A few blowflies buzzed about, looking for the blood.

Jelka's thickened lips tried to smile. 'Did you have any breakfast at all?'

'No,' he said. 'None at all.'

'Well, then, I'll fry you up some eggs.' She struggled painfully to her feet.

'Let me help you,' he said. 'I'll help you get your shirtwaist off. It's drying stuck to your back. It'll hurt.'

'No. I'll do it myself.' Her voice had a peculiar resonance* in it. Her dark eyes dwelt warmly on him for a moment, and then she turned and limped into the house.

Jim waited, sitting on the edge of the water-trough. He saw the smoke start out of the chimney and sail straight up into the air. In a few moments Jelka called him from the kitchen door.

'Come, Jim. Your breakfast.'

Four fried eggs and four thick slices of bacon lay on a warmed plate for him. 'The coffee will be ready in a minute,' she said.

'Won't you eat?'

'No. Not now. My mouth's too sore.'

He ate his eggs hungrily and then looked up at her. Her black hair was combed smooth. She had on a fresh white shirtwaist. 'We're going to town this afternoon,' he said. 'I'm going to order lumber.* We'll build a new house farther down the canyon.'

Her eyes darted to the closed bedroom door and then back to him. 'Yes,' she said. 'That will be good.' And then, after a moment, 'will you whip me any more — for this?'

'No, not any more, for this.'

Her eyes smiled. She sat down on a chair beside him, and Jim put out his hand and stroked her hair and the back of her neck.

John Steinbeck: The Murder 97

Glossary

The meanings given below are those which the words and phrases have as they occur in the story.

Page
85 *range*: line of mountains.
85 *spurs and ridges*: particular areas of mountainous ground with valleys between.
85 *arroyos*: (Spanish) narrow valleys cut by streams.
85 *canyons*: deep, narrow valleys with steep, high sides.
85 *buttressed*: a buttress is a stone structure built against a wall to make it stronger.
85 *Crusaders*: European soldiers of the Medieval period who invaded and occupied parts of the Middle East.
85 *strange accident . . . sandstone*: the stone of the mountain had been worn away over the centuries so that it looked exactly like a real castle.
85 *ranch*: cattle farm.
85 *warped*: twisted out of its original shape.
85 *defying*: showing they are not afraid of.
85 *No Trespassing*: you may not walk on this land; it is private property.
85 *morbid*: interested in dark things and especially death.
85 *forbids*: does not allow.
85 *plump*: slightly fat in an attractive way.
85 *awe*: feeling of great respect because of his power.
86 *manger-rack*: place for animal food.
86 *his majority*: becoming 21 and so a full adult.
86 *doe*: a female deer.
86 *startled*: surprised.
86 *bleary and bloated*: the beer had made his eyes dull and his face unusually fat-looking.
86 *suggestively*: in a way that showed that he meant something he had not spoken about.
86 *He*: the father's English is not very good.
86 *He's not like a man*: i.e., She won't like a man . . .
86 *passages of Scripture*: parts of the Bible.
86 *never wanted for any habitual thing*: never had to wait or ask for anything.

98 Conflict

- 86 *covered*: as if hiding something.
- 87 *interminable*: endless.
- 87 *range*: the land on which the cattle were kept.
- 87 *get in touch*: communicate.
- 87 *life apart*: a separate, individual life.
- 87 *whimpered*: made small, quiet crying noises.
- 87 *lapsed into*: went back again to being.
- 87 *crave*: want very much, long for.
- 87 *shame-sharpened vulgarity*: rough talk, especially about sex, which he enjoyed more because he felt it was wrong for him as a married man.
- 88 *put . . . buckboard*: attached the horses to the cart.
- 88 *giggle*: laugh in a silly way.
- 88 *holy picture tacked*: religious picture nailed.
- 88 *flat*: field.
- 88 *mower tumbled the last band*: cutter cut the last area.
- 89 *hitch up a rig*: attach horses to a kind of small cart.
- 89 *dusk*: the time of half darkness between day and night.
- 89 *halter*: leather strap for the horse's head.
- 90 *bay gelding*: reddish-brown horse.
- 90 ****: the following lines (ll. 2-8) describe how he caught the horse and fitted the bridle (leather head straps) and saddle (seat) to the horse. The details are not important.
- 90 *carbine*: a kind of gun.
- 90 *rammed . . . magazine*: pushed bullets into the gun.
- 90 *shimmered*: shone gently with light.
- 90 *roosters crowed*: cockerels (male chickens) called out.
- 91 *springboard*: high place where a small stream begins.
- 91 *brand*: mark of ownership made on skin with hot metal.
- 91 *stilted*: shortened (the moon is now higher in the sky).
- 91 *hogback*: smooth, rounded hill.
- 91 *coyotes*: a coyote is a kind of wolf.
- 92 *hoofbeats*: sound of horses' feet.
- 92 *bit*: metal part of a bridle which goes into the mouth.
- 92 *cinch*: leather strap attaching the saddle to the horse.
- 92 *horse-trough*: container for animals to drink from.
- 93 *peered*: looked hard.
- 93 *twitched*: suddenly moved a little.

John Steinbeck: The Murder 99

93 *smothered sobs*: sounds of crying he tries to control and hide.
93 *stirred the moon*: broke up the reflection of the moon.
94 *cocked*: prepared for firing.
94 *gurgled*: the noise of air passing through liquid in a narrow place.
94 *buckboard and pair*: kind of cart with two horses.
94 *sheriff*: officer of the law; a kind of policeman.
94 *coroner*: official who decides the legal cause of sudden or unexpected deaths.
94 *wrought up*: nervous and upset.
94 *tend to*: look after.
95 *sauntered away*: walked off in a casual, relaxed way.
95 *comforter*: bed cover.
95 *statement*: written account of what happened.
95 *dismissed*: cancelled.
95 *reluctantly*: in an unwilling way.
95 *bandana*: neck-cloth.
96 *resonance*: rich, full sound.
96 *lumber*: logs of wood for building.

Questions

1. If the story didn't have a title, what clues are there in the first page which would make you expect it to be about something strange and dark?

    (a) Is the countryside pleasant and friendly, or dramatic and a bit frightening? (p. 85)
    (b) What is the condition of the group of buildings below the 'castle'? (p. 85)
    (c) What is Jim's attitude to his property? Does the house matter very much to him? (p. 85)
    (d) How do people regard Jim? (p. 85)
    (e) Who goes with him to town? (p. 85)

2. Why does Jim marry Jelka? (p. 86)

    (a) Did he want to marry someone of a nationality different from his own?

100 Conflict

    (b) Was he a close friend of her family?
    (c) What was Jelka like physically?

3. What kind of relationship do Jim and Jelka have?

    (a) Does he take her father's advice seriously? (p. 86)
    (b) Is Jelka a good housekeeper? (p. 86)
    (c) Do she and Jim talk a lot and is she good company for him? (pp. 86—87)
    (d) What does Jelka remind Jim of and why? (p. 87)
    (e) Is their physical relationship really satisfying for them both? (p. 87)

4. What changes take place after the first few months of the marriage? (pp. 87—88)

    (a) Is Jim content with Jelka's company? (p. 87)
    (b) What old habit does Jim start again? (p. 87)
    (c) Has Jelka made friends in the neighbourhood? Who does she visit and how often? (p. 88)
    (d) Is Jim satisfied with Jelka's way of life?
    (e) Is Jelka moving towards Jim's outlook and way of life?
    (f) What does Jim want to know and how does Jelka answer him? (p. 88)

5. What is the situation on the Saturday night?

    (a) Where does Jim decide to go and when does he say he will return? (p. 88, p. 90)
    (b) At first, does he wish to be alone? (p. 89)
    (c) What does Jelka say she will do? (p. 89)
    (d) Why does Jim never get to Monterey? Who does he meet on the road and what is he told? (pp. 90—91)

6. How does Jim feel and act when he gets home?

    (a) What makes him suspicious? (p. 92)
    (b) When does he realize what is going on? Has he been at all suspicious before? (p. 92)
    (c) Does he shoot the other man in anger as soon as he sees him? (p. 93)
    (d) How does he feel when he goes out again and sits on the water-trough? (p. 93)

John Steinbeck: The Murder 101

- (e) What does he do in the time after he has shot Jelka's cousin? (p. 94)
- (f) What does he decide to do to Jelka and what effect does this have? (pp. 95—96)

7. What picture of their marriage do we get from the story?

    (a) What does Jim do whenever he spends the night in Monterey and does he appear to think his way of life is unfair to Jelka? (p. 87, p. 88)
    (b) How, in general, does he treat her?
    (c) Does Jelka mind when Jim goes away? How does she react when he suggests that someone might come while he is away? (p. 88)
    (d) When he sets off for Monterey, where does Jelka decide to sit? What reason does she give? Is it convincing? What is the real reason? (p. 89)
    (e) Does Jelka accept the death of her cousin quietly? (pp. 94—96)
    (f) What does she offer to do after Jim has beaten her and what is the meaning of this exchange?

    > 'Will you whip me any more — for this?'
    > 'No, not any more, for this.'   (p. 96)

8. What differences are there in the ways Jim and Jelka think about unfaithfulness?

    (a) Does Jelka know where Jim goes at nights? (p. 88)
    (b) Does she seem to mind?
    (c) Does Jim suspect Jelka of being unfaithful to him?
    (d) What does he do when he discovers the truth?

9. What do you think?
   In the first year of their marriage Jim was gentle to Jelka and each was unfaithful to the other. After he had murdered her lover and beaten her, she presumably remained faithful and the marriage appears to have been successful (p. 85). Which of the following do you agree or disagree with and why?

    (a) If you marry a foreigner, you must treat him/her in a foreign way.

- (b) Jim was a bully.
- (c) Jim was forced to act as he did and the results were good.
- (d) Jelka is an unfortunate victim of her own culture, which taught her to expect violence from men as the right thing.
- (e) Jim was right to beat Jelka.
- (f) Jim should have gone on being gentle to Jelka.
- (g) It was all Jelka's fault for sleeping with her cousin.
- (h) It was all Jim's fault for not staying at home.
- (i) The coroner and the sheriff were right to think as they did about the murder.
- (j) Jim and Jelka's marriage turned out to be a good one.
- (k) They should never have got married in the first place.

10. In many societies an unfaithful wife is, or has been, thought much worse and punished much more than an unfaithful husband. What does this show about such societies and what do you think about it?

* * * * *

1. In each story, when did you first suspect that there would be a murder?

2. Do you find you can believe in the Moores and the Fosters as people who might have been real?

3. Were Jim and Mrs Foster right to do what they did? How would you have acted if you had been them?

4. Does violence 'clear the air' and solve problems or does it just produce more problems and violence?

Barriers

Lesley Rowlands (1925—)

An Australian writer, who spent some years abroad and has written two books about her experiences, 'Why Can't the English?' (1959) and 'On Top of the World' (1961). She has also written a novel, 'A Bird in the Hand' (1965), and a number of short stories which have been published in magazines and anthologies. 'A Really Splendid Evening' was originally published in a magazine in 1963 and has since been reprinted in 'Best Australian Short Stories' (eds. D. Stewart & B. Davis), published in 1975 by Rigby.

The story

Whilst in Australia, Rao, a young Indian technician, pays a visit to the home of the wealthy Greenbergs. The story describes what happens on that 'really splendid evening'.

A Really Splendid Evening

'He's just as ghastly* as we thought he'd be,' the boy shouted in a hoarse* whisper up the stairs, and his words reached the visitor waiting in the front room. Or enough of them for him to wonder what the boy had meant. He heard 'he' and 'ghastly', but he didn't know what it was, didn't hear it properly, and he thought the boy must have said 'ghostly'. He glanced down at himself, sitting in the glazed chintz chair.

He didn't *look* ghostly. His hands were folded neatly in his lap, his legs quite elegantly crossed. His brown suit had been made at home and he realized now that perhaps the man who had made it had cheated him, saved a bit on the lapels,* which were not quite wide enough. But his shoes more than made up for* the suit. They were very light tan — almost golden, and they sparkled and twinkled in the late evening light coming through the windows. His cousin had purchased them in London, they were of the very best quality, though perhaps too narrow for his feet. His socks were a very dark maroon, and he had a handkerchief, pure silk, to match, in his top pocket. He put up a hand to make sure his hair had not become in any way disarranged. It hadn't. He really couldn't imagine why the boy should call him ghostly. He didn't feel like a ghost at all. He considered himself, in fact, a perfect gentleman.

Unaware of this, they kept him waiting for half an hour. He had begun to get restive,* and when they came into the room they found him giving his shoes a polish with a small piece of yellow cloth, a shoe polisher, which he always kept neatly folded in his trouser pocket for emergencies. Now he thrust it, hurriedly and clumsily, hoping they had not seen, into his coat pocket, where it made a small bulge.

He got up quickly and plunged* across the room towards the tall, elegant woman and the shorter, stoutish* man. He offered them his hand, in the friendly fashion that was his custom, and pumped hers heartily up and down,* making a small indentation* in his own from her rings.

105

'This is indeed a very happy occasion,' he said, for that is what he had decided to say, while he was waiting. It sounded even better than he had hoped, so he said it again.

'So glad you could come,' the woman said, after her husband had introduced them, and she trailed* away from him, in a bored way, to a cigarette box on a low table.

'Sorry to keep you waiting,' the man said, and he, too, walked away — to a small box in one corner of the room.

'No, no, not at all. It is my fault, entirely.' He sat down in the middle of the room, and watched his host and hostess busying themselves on either side of him, although some distance away. He didn't know why it was his fault. He'd arrived at six, at the time they'd asked him to come.* But he said, 'It was entirely my fault. I arrived early.'

'Oh? You didn't have any trouble finding your way?' Marie Greenberg was standing now quite near him, an unlighted cigarette waving aimlessly from her right fingers. He jumped to his feet again, saw some matches on the mantlepiece, and, with an explosive burst of flame, lit her cigarette. She collapsed wearily on to a chair and he looked at her shoes as he said, 'Not at all. In fact, quite the opposite. When I arrive in any big city I generally purchase a map. Then I have no trouble. It is not even necessary to request directions from passers-by.'

'How clever,' she murmured, as her husband came towards them, a silver tray in his hands.

'I've made martinis. That okay for you, Rao?' The three glasses were arranged in a triangle on the tray, the pale liquid almost level with the rims.

'Orange juice, if it is convenient,' he said. The sight of Greenberg with a tray in his hand had made him forget he was the host. He looked, rather round and dark, perspiring a little in the warm air, a little like a waiter, a steward.

'Oh, pardon. If you have it? Or water? A glass of fresh, iced water, perhaps?'

'Sorry. You don't drink, I take it?'

'Thank you, no. I have never in my whole life touched one single drop of alcoholic beverage.' He said this proudly, expecting exclamations of surprise and possibly incredulity* to fall from their lips, but they looked rather strongly disapproving, and Greenberg called his son to get a glass of orange juice from the kitchen.

They sat idly, waiting for this to come before they could raise their frail* glasses to their lips, before the evening could get under way.* She, still looking disapproving, gazed at the end of her cigarette, which she had not yet started to smoke. Harry was bad-tempered because he hadn't yet had his first drink of the day, had been called in early from tinkering with* his car to get ready for their guest, thought the guest impudent* anyway to have presumed on the hour they once spent* in each other's company at New Delhi airport. Rao was quiet because he didn't know what Australians talked about, at this hour of the day, or when visiting each other at any time. There was much he wanted to discuss, to tell them, questions he was hoping they would ask him. He thought, sadly, of visits at home — the shout of voices, the excitement, the many people coming and going.

The boy came with the orange juice, and released them.

'Cheers!'

'Cheers!'

'Cheerio!'

A little silence fell around them like a cloak. He groped his way out of its folds.*

'You have a very nice place here. Damn fine. Everything is just so.'

'Glad you like it. It's handy.' Harry didn't say to or for what. 'Have a good trip?' He went on. The martini had reached his elbows. A good sign.

'Ah, yes. The aeroplane was delaying in Singapore, but I was able to make some purchases there to send home to my wife.'

'Oh, are you married, Mr Rao? I didn't know. Harry didn't tell me.'

'I didn't know,' Harry said. 'You weren't married when I met you, were you?' he asked, remembering the airport, the heat, the warmish orange juice.

'No, no. I have married recently, since we met.'

'Well, congratulations.'

'Many thanks.'

'And is your wife living by herself during the time you'll be here?'

'Oh, no. No, no.' He was vehement* enough and would have been more so if he could have imagined a house, a flat, even a room, with one person, a woman, his wife, in it alone. This was beyond his imagination. He thought perhaps they were joking.

'She's living with my people. My father and mother, and my sisters.'

'And what did you buy her in Singapore?' Marie asked.

'Oh, some jewellery, one pair of slippers. She asked for one silver bracelet, but they were too costly.'

Harry put down his glass. 'Time for another?' he began, but caught his wife's eye. 'Perhaps not. Shall we go? Don't want to be late for our table.' He snapped off one of the lights, took his wife's fur from a chair in the hall, and put it gently round her shoulders. He'd paid a lot of money for that fur, didn't want it handled roughly. They stood for a few seconds at the front door, and Rao said:

'Pardon, may I know where the lavatory is?' In the small, astonished silence that followed, he heard the boy's half-muffled snort of laughter* somewhere beyond the hall.

'I have drunk many cups of tea and one glass of orange juice this afternoon, so my need is pressing,'* he said, wishing to stifle* their surprise with an explanation, and Harry made a gesture towards a door farther down the hall.

'It's certainly going to be a fascinating evening,' she said, as soon as he had left them and they had stepped, discreetly,* across the threshold* and out on to the porch, a little distance away from the offending door.

'How could I know he'd ring? Or even come to Australia for that matter? He was kind to me once, though I suppose he was under orders from Krisnam, who couldn't come himself.'

He remembered, again, the airport, and Rao bobbing about* playing the host. He'd certainly made things easy — got drinks, though warm, made porters and stewards and airport officials scurry round and be helpful too. He'd even changed some of his Indian currency, and, finally, loaded him with rather garish-looking* magazines to read on the plane.

'I can't think how you ever came to give him your address at all.'

'How could I know he'd ever turn up here?' he repeated, but she only looked at him, coldly, and then up at the stars. She would never give her address to anyone, anywhere in the world, she did not wish to meet again.

'You'd better get the car,' she said, and tapped her long pointed shoe lightly on the tiles.

The car was very large and quite black. Rao felt gay now, with relief, and told them in some detail of his recent trip — for this was the only thing they seemed to be interested in — dwelling on the food and the comfort of the aeroplane.

'They had every single thing in that aeroplane,' he said. 'Every old thing.' He caught a waft of Marie's perfume and tried to find the knob for winding down the window.

He was not an easy man to entertain, and, heaven knew, they were used to entertaining all sorts of people, Marie thought, as she emerged from the powder room* and found them waiting for her. Not even handsome, she mused* bitterly, as she followed the waiter down the avenue of tables. She nodded her head slightly, on its long stalk of neck, at several acquaintances, furious with Harry that he'd chosen this place to have dinner with an Indian who so obviously was not a prince.

Ordering the meal was an ordeal* they all wanted to forget as quickly as possible. Rao had never seen such large menus — whilst they were reading them they became quite isolated from each other, like people suddenly retiring into monasteries.* And he did not understand French,* so that they had to explain it to him, because of course he must know what every single thing was, in case he missed something he wanted to try. In the end he ordered plain roast chicken. Marie found this particularly irritating. Harry ordered some more martinis and orange juice while they were waiting.

'And how long have you been in Australia?' Marie asked, when the drinks arrived. She could hardly have cared less about the reply, which didn't answer her question.

'I have seen a number of beautiful places. Although I have only visited this State. Australia is a fine place. We all love Australia, in my country.'

'Really?' said Harry.

'Yes, yes. We love the U.K. best, naturally. But next to the U.K. we love your country. And we love your Mr Casey like any old thing.' He pronounced the name Casee, for almost every single syllable he uttered bore the wrong stress.

'Really?' Harry said again; and Marie said, 'And what exactly are you doing here, Mr Rao?'

'I am here to study deckniks,'* he replied, and, seeing her questioning eyebrows, repeated, 'Deckniks. I am a decknician.'

'Deckniks?' she asked.

'Yes, yes. I have come here for the purpose of studying deckniks. My firm is a management decknik firm. Deckniks. . . .'

'Oh,' she said. 'Yes. Deckniks. How interesting.' For she thought she was a lady to the tips of her pointed shoes, which she never had to have heeled.*

When the food arrived there was more trouble. Several waiters were needed to bring it, and some of them wheeled little trolleys with things cooking on them. It looked like a bazaar,* but the smell was different. He tried to help himself, but the condescending* waiter pushed his hands aside, without actually touching them, and served the food himself. There were too many knives and forks and spoons to know for sure which would be the right ones, so he tried to remember the stories his cousin had told him of dining out in London. When he began, at last, to eat, he had taken up the wrong knife, but he did not notice this himself, and called loudly for the waiter. He called so loudly that Marie and Harry, heads over food, jumped, and the waiter, four feet away, waited just five seconds before coming to bend over Harry.

'You wanted something, sir?'

'I . . .'

'Some iced water,' Rao commanded.

'Iced water, sir?' Harry knew the insult was not meant for him, but he flushed as if it had been.

'You'd like some iced water, Rao? Yes, please, waiter.'

Marie stared up at the chandeliers* and decided that tonight would be a good time to re-open the question of her new car.

'It's strange, in a restaurant such as this one — it has every damn thing, but no iced water,' Rao said gaily. 'I always insist on water at my table. Everywhere I go.'

'Really, Mr Rao? And I expect you have travelled widely?' she asked.

'In my country I travel many times a year. I make journeys for my firm. Usually I travel to many interesting places.'

'And abroad?' she probed.*

'This is my first journey abroad. But my father, R. K. Rao, has been many times in the U.K. And my cousin.'

'How fascinating,' she breathed. 'Next time you must bring your wife.'

He glanced at her. She certainly had funny ideas about wives.

'My wife would not wish to come,' he said. 'She has her work. She is a teacher,' he finished, proudly.

Marie couldn't think of anything more boring than a teacher. She was glad when the waiter appeared, tardily,* with the iced water. Mr Rao had dropped a large piece of chicken onto the tablecloth, and the headwaiter, a man they knew well, hurried over with a big white table napkin, and placed it over the offending stain, practically re-setting the table. It was very humiliating.

'And what have you been doing since you arrived?' she asked. Harry had withdrawn completely from them, and she felt that something must be said between now and the remote* time when they would be able to get up and leave.

'I have been very busy, generally, with my work,' Rao replied. 'And in my free time I have visited some scenic spots. I have been to the mountains, where many foreign tourists are rushing at the week-end. It was cold at the mountain resort but I was well muffled up. I purchased a muffler* specially for the journey.'

Marie, waving to friends, only heard half of this — something about a muffler, and wondered vaguely what it was: a word she knew well, and couldn't be bothered placing.

'How terribly embarrassing for you,' she said, 'to have a muffler,' for she decided, at last, that it might be some kind of silencer — for a gun?* — though it was hard to understand why he should have to carry a gun, and at the mountains. It would be too tiresome to try to find out.

For his part, Rao could not understand why a muffler was

embarrassing. Perhaps it was not done to wear one. Or had he made some other kind of mistake while he was speaking to her? He couldn't for his very life think what it might be. He wondered when he would be able to stop exchanging inanities* with this tall, superior woman, when Greenberg would start talking to him about interesting topics — politics, business management, the international situation — when they would be able to bang on the table, glare at each other, shout. But Harry, his head down, was immersed in his food. He hardly seemed to be there at all. Mr Rao put his head down too, and became immersed in his own rather tasteless meal.

He did not spill anything else on the tablecloth, and he only once more used the wrong knife, but the dinner, far from getting better, trailed feebly to a dismal cup of coffee.*

'It's a very funny thing,' he said, and he threw back his head and laughed quite loudly, for he did think it a very funny thing, 'you are white and you take black coffee and I am black, but I like my coffee to be white.'

'Very, very amusing,' she said.

They dropped him at his hotel, a shabby* little one they took some time to find. As he put his head in her window to say good night they caught each other's smell. She sank back a little, overpowered by oil on hair, by something else she had never encountered, which was not the odour of his body, and yet was. And he caught, again, her perfume, which sickened him, and her winebreath, and the sweetness emanating from her fur and her dress. They retreated from each other, while Harry drummed his fingers on the wheel and eased his foot on the brake.

'. . . a really splendid evening. I am most grateful,' he said, thinking of the long silences there had been in the restaurant, and wondering why he was grateful. At least the dinner had cost him nothing. Not a single farthing.*

'Not at all. A pleasure. Nice to see you again,' Harry said, clenching* and unclenching his leg muscle.

'Now. One evening perhaps I may offer you some hospitality? Would you like to come and see me? Perhaps I can give you some snacks?'

'That would be nice. Harry and I are going away for a month, but when we return. . . .'

'Before you go? Tomorrow?' He didn't mean any of this, and actually allowed his eyes to follow a couple along a dark street while he was speaking.

'Oh, no. We're . . . we're dining out tomorrow. When we come back . . . you ring us, that's the best thing.'

'Oh, sure,' he said, 'sure, sure. Pardon?'

'You ring us,' she repeated, grimly,* between her closed teeth, and Harry at length, transferred his foot to the accelerator. It was a powerful car, and as it jumped off it brushed him a little to one side. He watched the red tail-lights winking at him from the corner, and then they disappeared.

As he went back to the hotel he knew that he would never see either of them again, but he thought he'd wait until the morning before deciding whether or not to pretend to himself that he would.

114 Barriers

Glossary

The meanings given below are those which the words and phrases have as they occur in the story.

Page
105 *ghastly*: awful; terrible.
105 *hoarse*: rough.
105 *lapels*: folded parts of a jacket that continue the collar at the front.
105 *more than made up for*: undoubtedly compensated for.
105 *restive*: restless.
105 *plunged*: moved suddenly and with force.
105 *stoutish*: rather heavy and thick.
105 *pumped hers heartily up and down*: he shook her hand very hard and enthusiastically. The Greenbergs would think it vulgar and ungentlemanly to shake hands in this way, especially with a woman.
105 *indentation*: mark.
106 *trailed*: walked in a tired way.
106 *at the time they'd asked him to come*: in Britain and Australia, and in some other countries influenced by British customs, it is traditionally thought polite to arrive later for dinner than the time for which you were invited.
106 *incredulity*: disbelief.
107 *frail*: thin, easily broken.
107 *get under way*: start.
107 *tinkering with*: making small adjustments and repairs to.
107 *impudent*: rude to those superior to him.
107 *presumed on the hour they once spent*: thought that such an unimportant meeting was sufficient reason for making contact again on a social basis.
107 *a little silence fell around them like a cloak. He groped his way out of its folds*: (metaphor) A cloak is a coat without arms. The silence made it difficult for him to carry on a relaxed conversation, just as it can be difficult to get your arms free when you are wearing a cloak.
108 *was vehement*: spoke very strongly.

Lesley Rowlands: A Really Splendid Evening 115

108 *half-muffled snort of laughter*: partly stopped sound of unpleasant laughter.
108 *pressing*: urgent.
108 *stifle*: stop; keep back.
108 *discreetly*: tactfully, so as not to cause embarrassment.
108 *threshold*: floor at the entrance to the front door.
108 *bobbing about*: moving about quickly here and there.
108 *garish-looking*: brightly coloured in a vulgar way.
109 *powder room*: ladies' cloakroom and toilets.
109 *mused*: thought to herself.
109 *ordeal*: difficult and exhausting experience.
109 *monasteries*: buildings where monks live.
109 *he did not understand French*: it is often though smart and sophisticated to have the menu in French.
110 *deckniks*: Rao's pronunciation of 'technics' (technical studies).
110 *heeled*: have the bottom part to the back of a shoe replaced.
110 *bazaar*: street market in India and other Eastern countries.
110 *condescending*: acting in a way that shows feelings of superiority.
110 *chandeliers*: expensive lights which hang from the ceiling, made of large numbers of lights and pieces of glass.
111 *probed*: asked in order to get more information.
111 *tardily*: after rather a long time.
111 *remote*: distant; far away.
111 *muffler*: a less common word for a scarf.
111 *silencer — for a gun?*: 'to muffle' can mean 'to silence', hence Mrs Greenberg's mistake.
112 *inanities*: empty, pointless remarks.
112 *trailed feebly to a dismal cup of coffee*: moved in a dull way to a cup of coffee which nobody enjoyed.
112 *shabby*: not very clean or smart.
112 *farthing*: worthless coin.
112 *clenching*: tightening.
113 *grimly*: said with great effort and not in a friendly way.

116 *Barriers*

Questions

1. What indications are there in the first few pages that the evening will not be a success?
    (a) What do the words of the Greenbergs' son at the very beginning of the story show? (p. 105)
    (b) Why is Rao kept waiting half an hour? (p. 105)
    (c) How do the Greenbergs react when Rao tells them he does not drink? How did he expect them to react? (pp. 106-7)
    (d) Is Harry pleased that Rao has arrived? (p. 107) Why/why not?
    (e) 'He thought, sadly, of visits at home.' (p. 107) What are the differences between a visit that might take place at Rao's home and this visit to the Greenbergs'? (p. 107)

2. What was the situation when Harry and Rao first met?
    (a) Where did Harry and Rao first meet? (p. 107)
    (b) Why did they meet? (p. 108)
    (c) How did Rao help Harry on that occasion? (p. 108)

3. What factors make the meeting between Harry and Rao at Harry's house different?
    (a) Who is the host this time?
    (b) Did Harry expect Rao to visit him? (p. 109)
    (c) Why did Harry give Rao his address? (pp. 108–109)
    (d) At the restaurant Rao hopes Harry will talk to him about 'politics, business management, the international situation.' (p. 112) Is it possible that these might have been topics of discussion at their first meeting? Why is Harry silent now?

4. In what ways are Harry and Marie a well-matched couple, and in what ways are they badly-matched?
    (a) What do Harry and Marie look like? (p. 105)
    (b) Would you say Harry or Marie was the more dominant partner in the marriage. See for example the conversation they have on the porch. (pp. 108–109)
    (c) What do these passages tell the reader about their marriage and their social values?

Lesley Rowlands: A Really Splendid Evening 117

'He . . . took his wife's fur from the chair in the hall and put it gently round her shoulders. He'd paid a lot of money for that fur, didn't want it handled roughly.' (p. 108)

'Marie stared up at the chandeliers and decided that tonight would be a good time to re-open the question of her new car.' (p. 110)

(d) At the restaurant Marie talks to Rao whilst Harry remains silent. Is Marie, then, more polite to Rao?

(e) Would the evening have been different if Marie had not been there?

5. In the Greenbergs' eyes, Rao makes many social mistakes. What 'mistakes' does he make on the following occasions; how do the Greenbergs react to them?

   (a) arriving on time. (p. 106)
   (b) shaking hands with Mrs Greenberg in an enthusiastic way. (pp. 105–106)
   (c) asking for a non-alcoholic drink. (pp. 106–107)
   (d) asking for the lavatory and giving the reason why he needs to go there. (p. 108)
   (e) shouting for the waiter. (p. 110)
   (f) dropping food on the tablecloth. (p. 111)

   Would any of Rao's 'mistakes' be considered impolite or embarrassing in your own country? What would be considered impolite?

   Have you experienced cultural problems in a foreign country? How have you reacted?

6. How far do you agree or disagree with the following statements?

   (a) The story is not really about the barriers between different cultures but about unsympathetic people.
   (b) The story is about class differences not racial differences.
   (c) Harry is a different man when he is away from home — Harry's problem is his wife.
   (d) Rao should learn more about western customs.
   (e) The Greenbergs should learn more about eastern customs.
   (f) Rao and the Greenbergs are just interested in different things.

Alan Paton (1903—)

Alan Paton was born in Pietermaritzburg, South Africa. He taught in schools in Natal province for eleven years and then became the principal of an African reformatory outside Johannesburg in 1935. His reformatory did not lock the boys behind gates and fences but was run along the lines of trust and respect. The successes and failures of Paton's experiment are depicted in some of the short stories in 'Debbie Go Home' (1961) from which 'A Drink in the Passage' is taken. In 1948 Paton resigned as principal and devoted himself to writing and the cause of racial equality in his homeland. His convictions are passionately expressed in his two famous novels, 'Cry, the Beloved Country' (1948) and 'Too Late the Phalarope' (1953).

The story

When van Rensberg, a South African white man, asks a black man home for a drink, he hopes that the barriers between black and white can be broken down. The problem, however, cannot be solved so easily.

A Drink in the Passage

In the year 1960 the Union of South Africa celebrated its Golden Jubilee,* and there was a nation-wide sensation when the one-thousand-pound prize for the finest piece of sculpture was won by a black man, Edward Simelane. His work, 'African Mother and Child', not only excited the admiration, but touched the conscience or heart or whatever it is, of white South Africa, and was likely to make him famous in other countries.

It was by an oversight* that his work was accepted, for it was the policy of the Government that all the celebrations and competitions should be strictly segregated.* The committee of the sculpture section received a private reprimand* for having been so careless as to omit the words "for whites only" from the conditions, but was told, by a very high personage it is said, that if Simelane's work "was indisputably the best," it should receive the award. The committee then decided that this prize must be given along with the others, at the public ceremony which would bring this particular part of the celebrations to a close.

For this decision it received a surprising amount of support from the white public, but in certain powerful quarters there was an outcry* against any departure from the 'traditional policies' of the country, and a threat that many white prize-winners would renounce* their prizes. However a crisis was averted, because the sculptor was 'unfortunately unable to attend the ceremony'.

'I wasn't feeling up to it,' Simelane said mischievously to me. 'My parents, and my wife's parents, and our priest, decided that I wasn't feeling up to it. And finally I decided so too. Of course Majosi and Sola and the others wanted me to go and get my prize personally, but I said, "boys, I'm a sculptor, not a demonstrator".'

'This cognac is wonderful,' he said, 'especially in these big glasses. It's the first time I've had such a glass. It's also the first time I've drunk a brandy so slowly. In Orlando* you develop a throat of iron, and you just put back your head and pour it down, in case the police should arrive.'

119

He said to me, 'This is the second cognac I've had in my life. Would you like to hear the story of how I had my first?'

You know the Alabaster Bookshop in von Brandis Street? Well, after the competition they asked me if they could exhibit my 'African Mother and Child'. They gave a whole window to it, with a white velvet backdrop, if there is anything called white velvet, and complimentary words, *black man conquers white world*.

Well somehow I could never go and look in that window. On my way from the station to the Herald office, I sometimes went past there, and I felt good when I saw all the people standing there, but I would only squint at it out of the corner of my eye.

Then one night I was working late at the Herald, and when I came out there was hardly anyone in the streets, so I thought I'd go and see the window, and indulge certain pleasurable human feelings. I must have got a little lost in the contemplation of my own genius,* because suddenly there was a young white man standing next to me.

He said to me, 'What do you think of that, mate?'* And you know, one doesn't get called 'mate' every day.

'I'm looking at it,' I said.

'I live near here,' he said, 'and I come and look at it nearly every night. You know it's by one of your own boys, don't you? See, Edward Simelane.'

'Yes, I know.'

'It's beautiful,' he said. 'Look at that mother's head. She's loving that child, but she's somehow watching too. Do you see that? Like someone guarding. She knows it won't be an easy life.'

He cocked his head on one side, to see the thing better.

'He got a thousand pounds for it,' he said. 'That's a lot of money for one of your boys. But good luck to him. You don't get much luck, do you?'

Then he said confidentially,* 'Mate, would you like a drink?'

Well honestly I didn't feel like a drink at that time of night, with a white stranger and all, and me still with a train to catch to Orlando.

'You know we black people must be out of the city by eleven,' I said.

'It won't take long. My flat's just round the corner. Do you speak Afrikaans?'*

'Since I was a child,' I said in Afrikaans.

'We'll speak Afrikaans then. My English isn't too wonderful. I'm van Rensburg. And you?'

I couldn't have told him my name. I said I was Vakalisa, living in Orlando.

'Vakalisa, eh? I haven't heard that name before.'

By this time he had started off, and I was following, but not willingly. That's my trouble, as you'll soon see. I can't break off an encounter.* We didn't exactly walk abreast,* but he didn't exactly walk in front of me. He didn't look constrained.* He wasn't looking round to see if anyone might be watching.

He said to me, 'Do you know what I wanted to do?'

'No,' I said.

'I wanted a bookshop, like that one there. I always wanted that, ever since I can remember. When I was small, I had a little shop of my own.' He laughed at himself. 'Some were real books, of course, but some of them I wrote myself. But I had bad luck. My parents died before I could finish school.'

Then he said to me, 'Are you educated?'

I said unwillingly, 'Yes.' Then I thought to myself, how stupid, for leaving the question open.

And sure enough he asked, 'Far?'

And again unwillingly, I said, 'Far.'

He took a big leap and said, 'Degree?'

'Yes.'

'Literature?'

'Yes.'

He expelled his breath, and gave a long 'ah'. We had reached his building, Majorca Mansions, not one of those luxurious places. I was glad to see that the entrance lobby was deserted. I wasn't at my ease. I don't feel at my ease in such places, not unless I am protected by friends, and this man was a stranger. The lift was at ground level, marked 'Whites only. Slegs vir Blankes'.* Van Rensburg opened the door and waved me in. Was he constrained? To this day I don't know. While I was waiting for him to press the button, so that we could get moving and away from that ground floor, he stood with his finger suspended over it, and looked at me with a kind of honest, unselfish envy.*

'You were lucky,' he said. 'Literature, that's what I wanted to do.'

He shook his head and pressed the button, and he didn't speak again until we stopped high up. But before we got out he said suddenly, 'If I had had a bookshop, I'd have given that boy a window too.'

We got out and walked along one of those polished concrete passageways, I suppose you would call it a stoep* if it weren't so high up, let's call it a passage. On the one side was a wall, and plenty of fresh air, and far down below von Brandis Street. On the other side were the doors, impersonal* doors, you could hear radio and people talking, but there wasn't a soul in sight. I wouldn't like living so high; we Africans like being close to the earth. Van Rensburg stopped at one of the doors, and said to me, 'I won't be a minute.' Then he went in, leaving the door open, and inside I could hear voices. I thought to myself, he's telling them who's here. Then after a minute or so, he came back to the door, holding two glasses of red wine. He was warm and smiling.

'Sorry there's no brandy,' he said. 'Only wine. Here's happiness.'

Now I certainly had not expected that I would have my drink in the passage. I wasn't only feeling what you may be thinking. I was thinking that one of the impersonal doors might open at any moment, and someone would see me in a 'white' building, and see me and van Rensburg breaking the liquor laws of the country.* Anger could have saved me from the whole embarrassing situation, but you know I can't easily be angry. Even if I could have been, I might have found it hard to be angry with this particular man. But I wanted to get away from there, and I couldn't. My mother used to say to me, when I had said something anti-white, 'Son, don't talk like that, talk as you are.' She would have understood at once why I took a drink from a man who gave it to me in the passage.

Van Rensburg said to me, 'Don't you know this fellow Simelane?'

'I've heard of him,' I said.

'I'd like to meet him,' he said. 'I'd like to talk to him.' He added in explanation, 'You know, talk out my heart to him.'

A woman of about fifty years of age came from the room beyond, bringing a plate of biscuits. She smiled and bowed to me. I took one of the biscuits, but not for all the money in the world could I have said to her 'dankie, my nooi,'* or that disgusting 'dankie, missus,' nor did I want to speak to her in English because her language was Afrikaans, so I took the risk of it and used the word 'mevrou'* for the politeness of which some Afrikaners would knock a black man down, and I said, in high Afrikaans,* with a smile and a bow too, 'Ek is u dankbaar, Mevrou.'*

But nobody knocked me down. The woman smiled and bowed, and van Rensburg, in a strained voice* that suddenly came out of nowhere, said, 'Our land is beautiful. But it breaks my heart.'

The woman put her hand on his arm, and said 'Jannie, Jannie.'

Then another woman and a man, all about the same age, came up and stood behind van Rensburg.

'He's a B.A.,' van Rensburg told them. 'What do you think of that?'

The first woman smiled and bowed to me again, and van Rensburg said, as though it were a matter for grief, 'I wanted to give him brandy, but there's only wine.'

The second woman said, 'I remember, Jannie. Come with me.'

She went back into the room, and he followed her. The first woman said to me, 'Jannie's a good man. Strange, but good.'

And I thought the whole world was mad, and getting beyond me, with me a black stranger being shown a testimonial* for the son of the house, with these white strangers standing and looking at me in the passage, as though they wanted for God's sake to touch me somewhere and didn't know how, but I saw the earnestness* of the woman who had smiled and bowed to me, and I said to her 'I can see that, Mevrou.'

'He goes down every night to look at the statue,' she said. 'He says only God could make something so beautiful, therefore God must be in the man who made it, and he wants to meet him and talk out his heart to him.'

She looked back at the room, and then she dropped her voice* a little, and said to me, 'Can't you see, it's somehow because it's a black woman and a black child?'

And I said to her, 'I can see that, Mevrou.'

She turned to the man and said of me, 'He's a good boy.'

Then the other woman returned with van Rensburg, and van Rensburg had a bottle of brandy. He was smiling and pleased, and he said to me, 'This isn't ordinary brandy, it's French.'

He showed me the bottle, and I, wanting to get the hell out of that place, looked at it and saw it was cognac. He turned to the man and said, 'Uncle, you remember? When you were ill? The doctor said you must have good brandy. And the man at the bottle-store said this was the best brandy in the world.'

'I must go,' I said. 'I must catch that train.'

'I'll take you to the station,' he said. 'Don't you worry about that.'

He poured me a drink and one for himself.

'Uncle,' he said, 'what about one for yourself?'

The older man said, 'I don't mind if I do,' and he went inside to get himself a glass.

Van Rensburg said, 'Happiness,' and lifted his glass to me. It was good brandy, the best I've ever tasted. But I wanted to get the hell out of there. I stood in the passage and drank van Rensburg's brandy. Then Uncle came back with his glass, and van Rensburg poured him a brandy, and Uncle raised his glass to me too. All of us were full of goodwill,* but I was waiting for the opening of one of those impersonal doors. Perhaps they were too, I don't know. Perhaps when you want so badly to touch someone you don't care. I was drinking my brandy almost as fast as I would have drunk it in Orlando.

'I must go,' I said.

Van Rensburg said, 'I'll take you to the station.' He finished his brandy, and I finished mine too. We handed the glasses to Uncle, who said to me, 'Good night my boy.' The first woman said, 'May God bless you,' and the other women bowed and smiled. Then van Rensburg and I went down in the lift to the basement, and got into his car.

'I told you I'd take you to the station,' he said. 'I'd take you home, but I'm frightened of Orlando at night.'

Alan Paton: A Drink in the Passage   125

We drove up Eloff Street, and he said, 'Did you know what I meant?' I knew that he wanted an answer to something, and I wanted to answer him, but I couldn't because I didn't know what that something was. He couldn't be talking about being frightened of Orlando at night, because what more could one mean than just that?

'By what?' I asked.

'You know,' he said, 'about our land being beautiful?'

Yes, I knew what he meant, and I knew that for God's sake he wanted to touch me too and he couldn't for his eyes had been blinded by years in the dark. And I thought it was a pity, for if men never touch each other, they'll hurt each other one day. And it was a pity he was blind, and couldn't touch me, for black men don't touch white men any more; only by accident, when they make something like 'Mother and Child'.

He said to me, 'What are you thinking?'

I said, 'Many things,' and my inarticulateness* distressed me, for I knew he wanted something from me. I felt him fall back, angry, hurt, despairing, I didn't know. He stopped at the main entrance to the station, but I didn't tell him I couldn't go in there. I got out and said to him, 'Thank you for the sociable evening.'

'They liked having you,' he said. 'Did you see that they did?'

I said, 'Yes, I saw that they did.'

He sat slumped in his seat, like a man with a burden of incomprehensible, insoluble grief.* I wanted to touch him, but I was thinking about the train. He said 'Good-night' and I said it too. We each saluted the other. What he was thinking, God knows, but I was thinking he was like a man trying to run a race in iron shoes, and not understanding why he cannot move.

When I got back to Orlando, I told my wife the story, and she wept.

We didn't speak for a long time.

Then I said, 'Even the angels would weep.'

'Don't weep,' he said. 'Write it.'

'Write it,' he said eagerly. 'Perhaps that way I could make amends.'*

Then after a time he said to me, 'Do you think we'll ever touch each other? Your people and mine? Or is it too late?'

But I didn't give him any answer. For though I may hope, and though I may fear, I don't really know.

Alan Paton: A Drink in the Passage 127

Glossary

The meanings given below are those which the words and phrases have as they occur in the story.

Page
119 *Golden Jubilee*: fiftieth anniversary of the independence of South Africa.
119 *oversight*: failure to notice something.
119 *segregated*: white and black people separated.
119 *reprimand*: official disapproval and complaint.
119 *outcry*: public protest.
119 *renounce*: officially give up.
119 *Orlando*: part of Soweto, a town outside Johannesburg built to house only black people.
120 *contemplation of my own genius*: thoughts about my sculpture and my own skill as a sculptor.
120 *mate*: a friendly and informal word to use when speaking to someone.
120 *confidentially*: way of speaking between two people who might share a secret.
121 *Afrikaans*: English and Afrikaans (a language developed from Dutch) are the two official languages of South Africa.
121 *encounter*: meeting.
121 *abreast*: side by side.
121 *constrained*: unnatural or uneasy.
121 *Slegs vir Blankes*: (*Afrikaans*) whites only.
122 *envy*: wanting something that somebody else has.
122 *stoep*: (*Afrikaans*) a covered area for sitting etc. along one side of a house.
122 *impersonal*: having no personal character.
122 *the liquor laws of the country*: in South Africa it is illegal to drink alcohol in public, and it would be highly illegal for a white man to offer a black man alcohol in a public place.
123 *dankie, my nooi*: (*Afrikaans*) thank you, Mrs. (the type of speech a black servant might be expected to use to a white woman.)
123 *mevrou*: (*Afrikaans*) madam.
123 *high Afrikaans*: Afrikaans used by an educated speaker.

128   *Barriers*

123   *Ek is u dankbaar, Mevrou*: I'm very grateful to you, madam.
123   *strained voice*: unnatural voice because the speaker feels tense and anxious.
123   *testimonial*: statement about somebody's qualities — here the words of the woman at the door about van Rensburg.
123   *earnestness*: seriousness; sincerity.
123   *dropped her voice*: spoke in a lower, quieter voice.
124   *goodwill*: friendly feeling.
125   *inarticulateness*: inability to speak my thoughts clearly and fluently.
125   *burden of incomprehensible, insoluble grief*: a heavy feeling of unhappiness that can neither be understood nor be got rid of.
125   *make amends*: put a wrong right.

Questions

1. What problems were caused by a black South African winning the sculpture competition? (p. 119)

   (a) What was the Government's normal policy concerning national competitions?
   (b) Will the ceremony be public or private? (p. 119)
   (c) What were the divisions of opinion whether Simelane should be given the prize or not? (p. 119)
   (d) How was the crisis avoided? (p. 119)

2. Simelane says he decided not to go to the prize-giving ceremony because 'I wasn't feeling up to it'. What does he really mean by this? (p. 119)

   (a) How does he say these words? (p. 119) Does he say them seriously or humorously?
   (b) Who decides he is not 'feeling up to it'? (p. 119)
   (c) In what situations might someone normally say 'I'm not feeling up to it'? Is it the same sort of situation here? Why do you think he uses these words here?
   (d) What might have happened if Simelane had decided to attend the prize-giving ceremony?

Alan Paton: A Drink in the Passage 129

3. Why did van Rensburg invite Simelane home and why did Simelane accept?

    (a) Who begins the conversation and who talks most? (p. 120)
    (b) Does van Rensburg or Simelane talk most about himself? Consider why.
    (c) What does van Rensburg see in the sculpture? (p. 120) Consider the woman at the doorway's explanation of why van Rensburg goes to look at the statue. (p. 123)
    (d) Do you think van Rensburg would have begun a conversation and invited home a white man he met for the first time?
    (e) Does Simelane want to have a drink at van Rensburg's flat? (p. 120)
    (f) Why does Simelane accept a drink in the corridor when it is plainly dangerous? What advice would his mother have given him if she had been there? (p. 122)

4. What indications are there that van Rensburg does not really understand what it is like to be a black man in South Africa?

    (a) In what situations is Simelane placed in danger?
    (b) Who is put in most danger, Simelane or van Rensburg?
    (c) What kind of feelings do you think Simelane and van Rensburg have in the passage outside van Rensburg's flat? Are they the same? (pp. 122–125)
    (d) Why wasn't Simelane invited in?
    (e) Why doesn't van Rensburg drive Simelane home? (p. 124)
    (f) Why can't Simelane go in the front entrance of the station? (p. 125) Why doesn't he mention it to van Rensburg?

5. Both van Rensburg and Simelane wish to understand each other and make some sort of contact. Why is the attempt a failure?

    (a) Does van Rensburg want greater racial equality?
    (b) Why is the drink in the passage so crucial to an understanding of van Rensburg?

(c) Consider these excerpts: 'he wanted to touch me too and he couldn't; for his eyes had been blinded by years in the dark.' (p. 125)
'I wanted to touch him, but I was thinking about the train.' (p. 125)
(d) The author gives his reason for writing the story. What is it? (p. 125)

* * * * *

1. In both stories there are barriers between different races. In each story consider whether the writer is criticizing one race more than the other.

2. What kinds of barriers have you encountered? (Language barriers in a foreign country/prejudices/stereotyping of your own nationality.)

Looking Back

James Joyce (1882—1941)

James Joyce, born in Dublin, Southern Ireland, is one of the most important writers of the twentieth century. His most famous novel, 'Ulysses', influenced many writers and marked a new development in modern fiction. Joyce's genius, however, was not recognised by all, and both 'Ulysses' and 'Dubliners' were rejected by many publishers who feared the writings were obscene. Neither books, although their stories take place in Dublin, were published in Ireland; 'Dubliners' appearing in England in 1914 and 'Ulysses' in Paris in 1922. Joyce himself broke away from his Irish background and spent most of his life in Europe. He wrote 'Dubliners' in Trieste, thinking back with wit and affection to Dublin and the people he had known there, but also creating a book which analysed without mercy the failings, self-deceptions and the conservatisms of the Dubliners he had left behind him.

Other works by Joyce are 'Exiles' (1916) his only published play, 'A Portrait of the Artist as a Young Man' (1916), a very personal autobiography, and 'Finnegans Wake' (1939) where Joyce's experimentations with the possibilities of the English language reach their peak.

The story

'Clay', a story in 'Dubliners', is about an evening in the life of Maria. For years she had been like a second mother to Alphy and Joe, the two boys she had once taken care of, but now the boys are grown men and have become bitter enemies. Maria returns to the household for a party that is being held that evening.

Clay is a type of soil that becomes thick and sticky when wet, but it is also associated with death and the covering of the dead with earth. The title refers to a party game in the story where the main character, Maria, puts her hand in a saucer of clay.

Clay

The matron* had given her leave to go out as soon as the women's tea was over, and Maria looked forward to her evening out. The kitchen was spick and span*: the cook said you could see yourself in the big copper boilers. The fire was nice and bright and on one of the side-tables were four very big barmbracks. These barmbracks seemed uncut; but if you went closer you would see that they had been cut into long thick even slices and were ready to be handed round at tea. Maria had cut them herself.

Maria was a very, very small person indeed, but she had a very long nose and a very long chin. She talked a little through her nose, always soothingly*: *'Yes, my dear,'* and *'No, my dear.'* She was always sent for when the women quarrelled over their tubs* and always succeeded in making peace. One day the matron had said to her:

'Maria, you are a veritable peace-maker!'

And the sub-matron and two of the Board ladies* had heard the compliment. And Ginger Mooney was always saying what she wouldn't do to the dummy who had charge of the irons* if it wasn't for Maria. Everyone was so fond of Maria.

The women would have their tea at six o'clock and she would be able to get away before seven. From Ballsbridge to the Pillar, twenty minutes; from the Pillar to Drumcondra,* twenty minutes; and twenty minutes to buy the things. She would be there before eight. She took out the purse with the silver clasps and read again the words *A Present from Belfast.** She was very fond of that purse because Joe had brought it to her five years before when he and Alphy had gone to Belfast on a Whit-Monday* trip. In the purse were two half-crowns and some coppers. She would have five shillings clear after paying tram fare. What a nice evening they would have, all the children singing! Only she hoped that Joe wouldn't come in drunk. He was so different when he took any drink.

Often he had wanted her to go and live with them; but she would have felt herself in the way (though Joe's wife was ever so nice with her) and she had become accustomed to the life of the laundry. Joe was a good fellow. She had nursed him and Alphy too; and Joe used often say:

'Mamma is mamma, but Maria is my proper mother.'

After the break-up at home* the boys had got her that position in the *Dublin by Lamplight* laundry, and she liked it. She used to have such a bad opinion of Protestants, but now she thought they were very nice people, a little quiet and serious, but still very nice people to live with. Then she had her plants in the conservatory* and she liked looking after them. She had lovely ferns and wax-plants and, whenever anyone came to visit her, she always gave the visitor one or two slips* from her conservatory. There was one thing she didn't like and that was the tracts on the walls;* but the matron was such a nice person to deal with, so genteel.*

When the cook told her everything was ready she went into the women's room and began to pull the big bell. In a few minutes the women began to come in by twos and threes, wiping their steaming hands in their petticoats and pulling down the sleeves of their blouses over their red steaming arms. They settled down before their huge mugs which the cook and the dummy filled up with hot tea, already mixed with milk and sugar in huge tin cans. Maria superintended the distribution of the barmbrack and saw that every woman got her four slices. There was a great deal of laughing and joking during the meal. Lizzie Fleming said Maria was sure to get the ring* and, though Fleming had said that for so many Hallow Eves,* Maria had to laugh and say she didn't want any ring or man either; and when she laughed her grey-green eyes sparkled with disappointed shyness and the tip of her nose nearly met the tip of her chin. Then Ginger Mooney lifted up her mug of tea and proposed Maria's health, while all the other women clattered with their mugs on the table, and said she was sorry she hadn't a sup of porter to drink it in.* And Maria laughed again till the tip of her nose nearly met the tip of her chin and till her minute* body nearly shook itself asunder,* because she knew that Mooney meant well, though of course she had the notions of a common woman.

But wasn't Maria glad when the women had finished their tea and the cook and the dummy had begun to clear away the tea-

James Joyce: Clay 135

things! She went into her little bedroom and, remembering that the next morning was a mass* morning, changed the hand of the alarm from seven to six. Then she took off her working skirt and her house-boots and laid her best skirt out on the bed and her tiny dress-boots beside the foot of the bed. She changed her blouse too and, as she stood before the mirror, she thought of how she used to dress for mass on Sunday mornings when she was a young girl; and she looked with quaint* affection at the diminutive* body which she had so often adorned. In spite of its years she found it a nice tidy little body.

When she got outside the streets were shining with rain and she was glad of her own brown waterproof. The tram was full and she had to sit on the little stool at the end of the car, facing all the people, with her toes barely touching the floor. She arranged in her mind all she was going to do and thought how much better it was to be independent and to have your own money in your pocket. She hoped they would have a nice evening. She was sure they would but she could not help thinking what a pity it was Alphy and Joe were not speaking. They were always falling out* now, but when they were boys together they used to be the best of friends; but such was life.

She got out of her tram at the Pillar and ferreted* her way quickly among the crowds. She went into Downes's cake-shop but the shop was so full of people that it was a long time before she could get herself attended to. She bought a dozen of mixed penny cakes, and at last came out of the shop laden with a big bag. Then she thought what else would she buy: she wanted to buy something really nice. They would be sure to have plenty of apples and nuts. It was hard to know what to buy and all she could think of was cake. She decided to buy some plumcake, but Downes's plumcake had not enough almond icing on top of it, so she went over to a shop in Henry Street. Here she was a long time in suiting herself, and the stylish young lady behind the counter, who was evidently a little annoyed by her, asked her was it wedding-cake she wanted to buy. That made Maria blush and smile at the young lady; but the young lady took it all very seriously and finally cut a thick slice of plumcake, parcelled it up and said:

'Two-and-four, please.'

She thought she would have to stand in the Drumcondra tram because none of the young men seemed to notice her, but an elderly gentleman made room for her. He was a stout gentleman and he wore a brown hard hat; he had a square red face and a greyish moustache. Maria thought he was a colonel-looking gentleman and she reflected how much more polite he was than the young men who simply stared straight before them. The gentleman began to chat with her about Hallow Eve and the rainy weather. He supposed the bag was full of good things for the little ones and said it was only right that the youngsters should enjoy themselves while they were young. Maria agreed with him and favoured him with demure nods and hems.* He was very nice with her, and when she was getting out at the Canal Bridge, she thanked him and bowed, and he bowed to her and raised his hat and smiled agreeably; and while she was going up along the terrace, bending her tiny head under the rain, she thought how easy it was to know* a gentleman even when he has a drop taken.*

Everybody said: 'O, here's Maria!' when she came to Joe's house. Joe was there, having come home from business, and all the children had their Sunday dresses on. There were two big girls in from next door and games were going on. Maria gave the bag of cakes to the eldest boy, Alphy, to divide and Mrs Donnelly said it was too good of her to bring such a big bag of cakes, and made all the children say:

'Thanks, Maria.'

But Maria said she had brought something special for papa and mamma, something they would be sure to like, and she began to look for her plumcake. She tried in Downes's bag and then in the pockets of her waterproof and then on the hallstand, but nowhere could she find it. Then she asked all the children had any of them eaten it — by mistake, of course — but the children all said no and looked as if they did not like to eat cakes if they were to be accused of stealing. Everybody had a solution for the mystery and Mrs Donnelly said it was plain that Maria had left it behind her in the tram. Maria, remembering how confused the gentleman with the greyish moustache had made her, coloured with shame and vexation* and disappointment. At the thought of the failure of her little surprise and of the two and fourpence she had thrown away for nothing she nearly cried outright.

But Joe said it didn't matter and made her sit down by the fire. He was very nice with her. He told her all that went on in his office, repeating for her a smart answer which he had made to the manager. Maria did not understand why Joe laughed so much over the answer he had made, but she said that the manager must have been a very overbearing* person to deal with. Joe said he wasn't so bad when you knew how to take him,* that he was a decent sort so long as you didn't rub him the wrong way.* Mrs Donnelly played the piano for the children and they danced and sang. Then the two next-door girls handed round the nuts. Nobody could find the nut-crackers, and Joe was nearly getting cross over it and asked how did they expect Maria to crack nuts without a nut-cracker. But Maria said she didn't like nuts and that they weren't to bother about her. Then Joe asked would she take a bottle of stout,* and Mrs Donnelly said there was port wine too in the house if she would prefer that. Maria said she would rather they didn't ask her to take anything: but Joe insisted.

So Maria let him have his way* and they sat by the fire talking over old times and Maria thought she would put in a good word for* Alphy. But Joe cried that God might strike him stone dead if ever he spoke a word to his brother again and Maria said she was sorry she had mentioned the matter. Mrs Donnelly told her husband it was a great shame for him to speak that way of his own flesh and blood,* but Joe said that Alphy was no brother of his and there was nearly being a row on the head of it.* But Joe said he would not lose his temper on account of the night it was, and asked his wife to open some more stout. The two next-door girls had arranged some Hallow Eve games and soon everything was merry again. Maria was delighted to see the children so merry and Joe and his wife in such good spirits.* The next-door girls put some saucers on the table and then led the children up to the table, blindfold. One got the prayer-book* and the other three got the water;* and when one of the next-door girls got the ring Mrs Donnelly shook her finger at the blushing girl as much as to say: *O, I know all about it!* They insisted then on blindfolding

138 *Looking Back*

Maria and leading her up to the table to see what she would get; and, while they were putting on the bandage, Maria laughed and laughed again till the tip of her nose nearly met the tip of her chin.

They led her up to the table amid laughing and joking, and she put her hand out in the air as she was told to do. She moved her hand about here and there in the air and descended on one of the saucers. She felt a soft wet substance with her fingers and was surprised that nobody spoke or took off her bandage. There was a pause for a few seconds; and then a great deal of scuffling* and whispering. Somebody said something about the garden, and at last Mrs Donnelly said something very cross* to one of the next-door girls and told her to throw it out at once: that was no play.* Maria understood that it was wrong that time and so she had to do it over again: and this time she got the prayer-book.

After that Mrs Donnelly played Miss McCloud's Reel* for the children, and Joe made Maria take a glass of wine. Soon they were all quite merry again, and Mrs Donnelly said Maria would enter a convent* before the year was out because she had got the prayer-book. Maria had never seen Joe so nice to her as he was that night, so full of pleasant talk and reminiscences.* She said they were all very good to her.

At last the children grew tired and sleepy and Joe asked Maria would she not sing some little song before she went, one of the old songs. Mrs Donnelly said '*Do, please, Maria!*' and so Maria had to get up and stand beside the piano. Mrs Donnelly bade the children be quiet and listen to Maria's song. Then she played the prelude and said '*Now, Maria!*' and Maria, blushing very much, began to sing in a tiny quavering* voice. She sang *I Dreamt that I Dwelt*, and when she came to the second verse she sang again:

> 'I dreamt that I dwelt in marble halls
>   With vassals and serfs* at my side,
> And of all who assembled within those walls
>   That I was the hope and the pride.
>
> 'I had riches too great to count; could boast
>   Of a high ancestral name,
> But I also dreamt, which pleased me most,
>   That you loved me still the same.'

But no one tried to show her her mistake; and when she had ended her song Joe was very much moved.* He said that there was no time like the long ago and no music for him like poor old Balfe,* whatever other people might say; and his eyes filled up so much with tears that he could not find what he was looking for and in the end he had to ask his wife to tell him where the cork-screw* was.

Glossary

The meanings given below are those which the words and phrases have as they occur in the story.

Page
- 133 *matron*: head housekeeper.
- 133 *spick and span*: bright, clean and tidy.
- 133 *soothingly*: in a voice that calms.
- 133 *tubs*: large vessels for washing clothes.
- 133 *the Board ladies*: the group of ladies who control the organisation of the laundry.
- 133 *dummy who had charge of the irons*: worker who was responsible for the irons.
- 133 *Ballsbridge, Pillar, Drumcondra*: parts of Dublin, Southern Ireland.
- 133 *Belfast*: the capital of Northern Ireland.
- 133 *Whit-Monday*: a national holiday in the seventh week after Easter.
- 134 *break-up at home*: division of the family through an argument.
- 134 *conservatory*: room with glass walls and roof where plants are kept.
- 134 *slips*: small pieces of a plant from which new plants can be grown.
- 134 *tracts on the walls*: short religious or moral comments, framed and hung like pictures on the walls.
- 134 *genteel*: polite and well-bred.
- 134 *Maria was sure to get the ring*: a reference to a game played at Hallowe'en (October 31st) in which someone is blindfolded (has his eyes covered with a handkerchief) and must feel for certain objects. If a ring is picked up it is a sign that the person will soon get married.
- 134 *Hallow Eves*: October 31st. The day before All Saints' Day.
- 134 *a sup of porter to drink it in*: some beer in order to drink to Maria's health.
- 134 *minute*: maɪnˈjuːt very small.
- 134 *shook itself asunder*: as though shaking herself to pieces through laughing so hard.

James Joyce: Clay 141

135 *mass*: Roman Catholic religious ceremony.
135 *quaint*: charmingly innocent.
135 *diminutive*: unusually small.
135 *falling out*: quarrelling.
135 *ferreted*: pushing through with small, active movements.
136 *demure nods and hems*: small movements and sounds of polite agreement.
136 *know*: recognize.
136 *has a drop taken*: (*Irish coll.*) has been drinking alcohol.
136 *vexation*: annoyance.
137 *overbearing*: over forceful.
137 *knew how to take him*: (*coll.*) understood his personality.
137 *rub him the wrong way*: (*idiom.*) irritate or anger him.
137 *stout*: dark coloured beer.
137 *let him have his way*: let him do what he wanted.
137 *put in a good word for*: say some good things about.
137 *his own flesh and blood*: his close relatives (his brother).
137 *a row on the head of it*: an argument about it.
137 *in such good spirits*: so happy.
137 *the prayer-book*: a sign that the person would lead a religious life.
137 *the water*: probably a sign that the person would travel overseas.
138 *scuffling*: moving around.
138 *cross*: angrily.
138 *that was no play*: that turn was not to be counted.
138 *Miss McCloud's Reel*: an Irish dance.
138 *convent*: building where nuns live and work.
138 *reminiscences*: talk of past experiences.
138 *quavering*: shaking.
138 *vassals and serfs*: farmers in the Middle Ages who did not own their land.
139 *very much moved*: filled with emotion.
139 *Balfe*: the writer of the song.
139 *cork-screw*: tool for removing corks from bottles.

142 *Looking Back*

Questions

1. What do you find out at the laundry about Maria's attitudes, people's attitudes to her, and her past history?
    (a) Is Maria popular at the laundry? (p. 133)
    (b) Why is she called the peacemaker? (p. 133)
    (c) What does Maria think of the women who work there? See her comment on Ginger Mooney. (p. 134)
    (d) The people who run the laundry are Protestants. Is Maria a Protestant? (p. 134, p. 135)
    (e) Why did Maria leave the house where she had lived and come to work at the laundry? (p. 134)
    (f) Do you think Maria was happier with the family she used to live with? Is she totally content at the laundry?

2. What details at the beginning of the story suggest the type of person Maria is?
    (a) What does Maria look like? (p. 133)
    (b) Is Maria young any more? (p. 133, p. 134)
    (c) Is she married or single?
    (d) When the laundry women talk about the party and say Maria will get the ring, she laughs with 'disappointed shyness'. Why 'disappointed'?
    (e) How does Maria react to the woman in the cake-shop (p. 135), and to the man in the tram? (p. 136) How do they help us to form a picture of Maria?

3. Why might her part in bringing up Alphy and Joe be so important to Maria, and how might she feel she has failed?
    (a) Maria nursed Alphy and Joe when they were young. Is she related to their family? (p. 134)
    (b) Is any mention made of Maria's own family?
    (c) 'Mamma is mamma, but Maria is my proper mother.' (p. 134) What does this show the reader about the closeness of Maria to the family? How do you think she felt when she decided to leave the family?
    (d) Maria is a peacemaker at the laundry. How does she try to be a peacemaker in the family? Does she succeed? (p. 137)

James Joyce: Clay 143

4. Underneath the surface happiness of the party there are sadder undertones. What are they?

   (a) When Maria arrives at the party she finds she has lost the parcel containing the cakes. Where did she lose it, and what might have made her forget it? How does she feel about losing it? (pp. 136—137)

   (b) In the party game the players feel for one of these objects: a prayer-book, a ring and a saucer of water. What does each of these signify?

   (c) The women at the laundry say Maria will get the ring. Has she ever chosen the ring? (p. 134) Is it likely that Maria will marry?

   (d) Why are people embarrassed when Maria puts her hand in the 'soft wet substance' (clay)? Would they be so embarrassed if one of the children had done the same?

   (e) Maria sings a song at the end of the story (p. 138) about the end of love in one partner and the continuing love of the other. How does Joe react to the song? How does Joe react when Maria talks about his brother Alphy? (p. 137) What conclusions do you come to about Joe's personality?

5. 'Clay' can be looked at from many points of view. Which of these themes do you think are most important, and why?

   (a) The story is about disappointment; what Maria deserves in life she does not get.

   (b) The story is about the break-up of a family and the effect it has on Maria.

   (c) The story concerns the stupidity of Joe who refuses to make friends with his brother.

   (d) The story is about people who cannot change their lives whether they would like to or not.

Perhaps there are themes in the story, not mentioned above, that you find important. What are they?

Katherine Mansfield (1888—1923)

Katherine Mansfield was born in New Zealand and came to England when she was in her twenties. After her first unsuccessful marriage, she married in 1913 the editor and critic, John Middleton Murry, who encouraged her in her writing. The death of her younger brother in France in 1915 made a lasting impression on her, and the memories of their childhood together in New Zealand are recreated in some of her short stories. Her stories normally deal with the details of everyday life and show a particular compassion for the lonely and the outsider in childhood, maturity and in old age. After a prolonged illness she died of tuberculosis at Fontainebleau in France at the age of 34. Her best-known collections of short stories include 'Bliss' (1921), 'The Garden Party' (1922) — from which this story is taken —, 'The Dove's Nest' (1923) and 'Something Childish' (1924).

The story

All his life Mr Neave has worked hard to pay for the luxuries his family have demanded. But now as he is about to retire, he begins to realize what sort of relationship he and his family have.

An Ideal Family

That evening for the first time in his life, as he pressed through the swing-door and descended the three broad steps to the pavement, old Mr Neave felt he was too old for the spring. Spring — warm, eager, restless — was there, waiting for him in the golden light, ready in front of everybody to run up, to blow in his white beard, to drag sweetly on his arm. And he couldn't meet her, no; he couldn't square up* once more and stride off, jaunty* as a young man. He was tired and, although the late sun was still shining, curiously cold, with a numbed feeling* all over. Quite suddenly he hadn't the energy, he hadn't the heart to stand this gaiety and bright movement any longer; it confused him. He wanted to stand still, to wave it away with his stick, to say, 'Be off with you!'* Suddenly it was a terrible effort to greet as usual — tipping his wide-awake* with his stick — all the people whom he knew, the friends, acquaintances, shopkeepers, postmen, drivers. But the gay glance that went with that gesture, the kindly twinkle* that seemed to say, 'I'm a match and more for any of you'* — that old Mr Neave could not manage at all. He stumped along, lifting his knees high as if he were walking through air that had somehow grown heavy and solid like water. And the homeward-going crowd hurried by, the trams clanked, the light carts clattered, the big swinging cabs* bowled along* with that reckless, defiant indifference* that one knows only in dreams . . .

It had been a day like other days at the office. Nothing special had happened. Harold hadn't come back from lunch until close on four. Where had he been? What had been up to? He wasn't going to let his father know. Old Mr Neave had happened to be in the vestibule,* saying goodbye to a caller, when Harold sauntered* in, perfectly turned out* as usual, cool, suave,* smiling that peculiar little half-smile that women found so fascinating.

Ah, Harold was too handsome, too handsome by far; that had been the trouble all along. No man had a right to such eyes, such lashes* and such lips; it was uncanny.* As for his mother, his sisters, and the servants, it was not too much to say they made a young god of him; they worshipped Harold, they forgave him everything; and he had needed some forgiving ever since the time when he was thirteen and he had stolen his mother's purse, taken the money, and hidden the purse in the cook's bedroom. Old Mr Neave struck sharply with his stick upon the pavement edge. But it wasn't only his family who spoiled Harold, he reflected, it was everybody; he had only to look and to smile, and down they went before him.* So perhaps it wasn't to be wondered at that he expected the office to carry on the tradition. H'm, h'm! But it couldn't be done. No business — not even a successful, established, big paying concern* — could be played with. A man had either to put his whole heart and soul into it,* or it went all to pieces* before his eyes . . .

And then Charlotte and the girls were always at him* to make the whole thing over to* Harold, to retire, and to spend his time enjoying himself. Enjoying himself! Old Mr Neave stopped dead under a group of ancient cabbage palms outside the Government buildings! Enjoying himself! The wind of evening shook the dark leaves to a thin airy cackle.* Sitting at home, twiddling his thumbs,* conscious all the while his life's work was slipping away, dissolving, disappearing through Harold's fine fingers, while Harold smiled . . .

'Why will you be so unreasonable, father? There's absolutely no need for you to go to the office. It only makes it very awkward for us when people persist in saying how tired you're looking. Here's this huge house and garden. Surely you could be happy in — in — appreciating it for a change. Or you could take up some hobby.'*

And Lola the baby chimed in loftily. 'All men ought to have hobbies. It makes life impossible if they haven't.'

Well, well! He couldn't help a grim* smile as painfully he began to climb up the hill that led into Harcourt Avenue. Where would Lola and her sisters and Charlotte be if he'd gone in for hobbies, he'd like to know? Hobbies couldn't pay for the town house and the seaside bungalow,* and their horses, and their golf, and the sixty-guinea* gramophone in the music-room for them to dance to. Not that he grudged* them these things. No, they were smart, good-looking girls, and Charlotte was a remarkable woman; it was natural for them to be in the swim.* As a matter of fact, no other house in the town was as popular as theirs; no other family entertained so much. And how many times old Mr Neave, pushing the cigar box across the smoking-room table, had listened to praises of his wife, his girls, of himself even.

'You're an ideal family, sir, an ideal family. It's like something one reads about or sees on the stage.'

'That's all right, my boy,' old Mr Neave would reply. 'Try one of those; I think you'll like them. And if you care to smoke in the garden, you'll find the girls out on the lawn, I dare say.'

That was why the girls had never married, so people said. They could have married anybody. But they had too good a time at home. They were too happy together, the girls and Charlotte. H'm, h'm! Well, well! Perhaps so . . .

By this time he had walked the length of fashionable Harcourt Avenue; he had reached the corner house, their house. The carriage gates were pushed back; there were fresh marks of wheels on the drive. And then he faced the big white-painted house, with its wide-open windows, its tulle* curtains floating outwards, its blue jars of hyacinths on the broad sills. On either side of the carriage porch* their hydrangeas — famous in the town — were coming into flower; the pinkish, bluish masses of flower lay like light among the spreading leaves. And somehow, it seemed to old Mr Neave that the house and the flowers, and even the fresh marks on the drive, were saying, 'There is young life here. There are girls —'

The hall, as always, was dusky* with wraps, parasols, gloves, piled on the oak chests. From the music-room sounded the piano, quick, loud and impatient. Through the drawing-room door that was ajar* voices floated.

'And were there ices?' came from Charlotte. Then the creak, creak of her rocker.*

'Ices!' cried Ethel. 'My dear mother, you never saw* such ices. Only two kinds. And one a common little strawberry shop ice, in a sopping wet frill.'*

'The food altogether was too appalling,' came from Marion.

'Still, it's rather early for ices,' said Charlotte easily.

'But why, if one has them at all . . .' began Ethel.

'Oh, quite so, darling,' crooned Charlotte.

148   *Looking Back*

Suddenly the music-room door opened and Lola dashed out.* She started,* she nearly screamed, at the sight of old Mr Neave.

'Gracious, father! What a fright you gave me! Have you just come home? Why isn't Charles here to help you off with your coat?'

Her cheeks were crimson from playing, her eyes glittered, the hair fell over her forehead. And she breathed as though she had come running through the dark and was frightened. Old Mr Neave stared at his youngest daughter; he felt he had never seen her before. So that was Lola, was it? But she seemed to have forgotten her father; it was not for him that she waited there. Now she put the tip of her crumpled handkerchief between her teeth and tugged at it angrily. The telephone rang. A-ah! Lola gave a cry like a sob* and dashed past him. The door of the telephone-room slammed, and at the same moment Charlotte called, 'Is that you, father?'

'You're tired again,' said Charlotte reproachfully,* and she stopped the rocker and offered him her warm plum-like cheek. Bright-haired Ethel pecked* his beard; Marion's lips brushed his ear.

'Did you walk back, father?' asked Charlotte.

'Yes, I walked home,' said old Mr Neave, and he sank into one of the immense drawing-room chairs.

'But why didn't you take a cab?' said Ethel. 'There are hundreds of cabs about at that time.'

'My dear Ethel,' cried Marion, 'if father prefers to tire himself out, I really don't see what business of ours it is to interfere.'

'Children, children?' coaxed Charlotte.

But Marion wouldn't be stopped. 'No mother, you spoil* father, and it's not right. You ought to be stricter with him. He's very naughty.' She laughed her hard, bright laugh and patted her hair in a mirror. Strange! When she was a little girl she had such a soft, hesitating voice; she had even stuttered,* and now, whatever she said — even if it was only 'Jam, please, father' — it rang out as though she were on the stage.

'Did Harold leave the office before you, dear?' asked Charlotte, beginning to rock again.

'I'm not sure. I didn't see him after four o'clock.'

'He said —' began Charlotte.

But at that moment Ethel, who was twitching over* the leaves of some paper or other, ran to her mother and sank down beside her chair.

'There, you see,' she cried. 'That's what I mean, mummy. Yellow, with touches of silver. Don't you agree?'

'Give it to me, love,' said Charlotte. She fumbled for her tortoise-shell spectacles and put them on, gave the page a little dab* with her plump small fingers, and pursed up* her lips. 'Very sweet!' she crooned* vaguely; she looked at Ethel over her spectacles. 'But I shouldn't have the train.'*

'Not the train!' wailed* Ethel tragically. 'But the train's the whole point.'

'Here, mother, let me decide.' Marion snatched the paper playfully from Charlotte. 'I agree with mother,' she cried triumphantly. 'The train overweights it.'

Old Mr Neave, forgotten, sank into the broad lap of his chair, and, dozing, heard them as though he dreamed. There was no doubt about it, he was tired out; he had lost his hold.* Even Charlotte and the girls were too much for him tonight. They were too . . . too . . . But all his drowsing* brain could think of was — too *rich* for him. And somewhere at the back of everything he was watching a little withered* ancient man climbing up endless flights of stairs. Who was he?

'I shan't dress tonight,' he muttered.

'What do you say, father?'

'Eh, what, what?' Old Mr Neave woke with a start and stared across at them. 'I shan't dress tonight,' he repeated.

'But, father, we've got Lucile coming, and Henry Davenport, and Mrs Teddie Walker.'

'It will look so *very* out of the picture.'*

'Don't you feel well, dear?'

'You needn't make any effort. What is Charles *for*?'

'But if you're really not up to it,' Charlotte wavered.*

'Very well! Very well!' Old Mr Neave got up and went to join that little old climbing fellow* just as far as his dressing-room . . .

There young Charles was waiting for him. Carefully, as though everything depended on it, he was tucking a towel round a hot-water can. Young Charles had been a favourite of his ever since as a little red-faced boy he had come into the house to look after the fires. Old Mr Neave lowered himself into the cane lounge* by the window, stretched out his legs, and made his evening joke, 'Dress him up, Charles!' And Charles, breathing intensely and frowning, bent forward to take the pin out of his tie.

H'm, h'm! Well, well! It was pleasant by the open window, very pleasant — a fine mild evening. They were cutting the grass on the tennis court below; he heard the soft churr of the mower. Soon the girls would begin their tennis parties again. And at the thought he seemed to hear Marion's voice ring out, 'Good for you, partner . . . Oh, *played*, partner . . . Oh, *very* nice indeed.' Then Charlotte calling from the veranda, 'Where is Harold?' And Ethel, 'He's certainly not here, mother.' And Charlotte's vague, 'He said —'

Old Mr Neave sighed, got up, and putting one hand under his beard, he took the comb from young Charles, and carefully combed the white beard over. Charles gave him a folded handkerchief, his watch and seals, and spectacle case.

'That will do, my lad.' The door shut, he sank back, he was alone . . .

And now that little ancient fellow was climbing down endless flights that led to a glittering, gay dining-room. What legs he had! They were like a spider's — thin, withered.

'You're an ideal family, sir, an ideal family.'

But if that were true, why didn't Charlotte or the girls stop him? Why was he all alone, climbing up and down? Where was Harold? Ah, it was no good expecting anything from Harold. Down, down went the little old spider, and then, to his horror, old Mr Neave saw him slip past the dining-room and make for the porch, the dark drive, the carriage gates, the office. Stop him, stop him, somebody!

Old Mr Neave started up. It was dark in his dressing-room; the window shone pale. How long had he been asleep? He listened, and through the big, airy, darkened house there floated far-away voices, far-away sounds. Perhaps, he thought vaguely, he had been asleep for a long time. He'd been forgotten. What had all this to do with him — this house and Charlotte, the girls and Harold —

what did he know about them? They were strangers to him. Life had passed him by. Charlotte was not his wife. His wife!

... A dark porch, half hidden by a passion-vine,* that drooped sorrowful, mournful, as though it understood. Small, warm arms were round his neck. A face, little and pale, lifted to his, and a voice breathed, 'Goodbye, my treasure.'*

My treasure! 'Goodbye, my treasure!' Which of them had spoken? Why had they said goodbye? There had been some terrible mistake. *She* was his wife, that little pale girl, and all the rest of his life had been a dream.

Then the door opened, and young Charles, standing in the light, put his hands by his side and shouted like a young soldier, 'Dinner is on the table, sir!'

'I'm coming, I'm coming,' said old Mr Neave.

Glossary

The meanings given below are those which the words and phrases have as they occur in the story.

Page
- 145 *square up*: stand straight.
- 145 *jaunty*: feeling confident.
- 145 *numbed feeling*: unable to feel sensations.
- 145 *Be off with you!*: Go away!
- 145 *tipping his wide-awake*: touching his hat (with his stick) as a way of greeting.
- 145 *twinkle*: bright look (in the eye).
- 145 *I'm a match and more for any of you*: I'm as good, if not better than any of you.
- 145 *cabs*: horse-drawn carriages hired for short journeys.
- 145 *bowled along*: went along quickly.
- 145 *reckless, defiant indifference*: the cab's speed showed the driver did not care about others' safety.
- 145 *vestibule*: entrance hall to the office.
- 145 *sauntered*: walked in an unhurried way.
- 145 *turned out*: dressed.
- 145 *suave*: with smooth, gracious manners.
- 145 *lashes*: eyelashes; hair on the edge of the eyelid.
- 145 *uncanny*: strange; unusual.
- 146 *down they went before him*: They behaved to him as if he were a god; they found him so attractive.
- 146 *big paying concern*: business that makes a lot of money.
- 146 *put his whole heart and soul into it*: take it completely seriously.
- 146 *went all to pieces*: failed, or was destroyed.
- 146 *were always at him*: always telling him.
- 146 *make the whole thing over to*: give the business to.
- 146 *cackle*: noise like a loud, unpleasant laugh.
- 146 *twiddling his thumbs*: (*idiom.*) doing nothing.
- 146 *hobby*: leisure-time occupation.
- 146 *grim*: serious.
- 146 *bungalow*: one-storey house.
- 146 *guinea*: an old coin worth about a pound.

146 *grudged*: was unwilling to give.
146 *be in the swim*: take a full part in up-to-date social and cultural activities.
147 *tulle*: thin material.
147 *porch*: roofed doorway at the entrance to a building.
147 *dusky*: dark.
147 *ajar*: slightly open.
147 *rocker*: rocking chair.
147 *you never saw*: an expression of surprise.
147 *sopping wet frill*: the paper decoration around the ice cream was very wet.
148 *dashed out*: ran out suddenly.
148 *started*: jumped; moved suddenly in surprise.
148 *sob*: sound made by breathing in sharply when crying.
148 *reproachfully*: finding fault.
148 *pecked*: kissed quickly with no affection.
148 *spoil*: pay too much attention to the comfort of.
148 *stuttered*: nervous repetition of the same sound when speaking.
149 *twitching over*: hurriedly turning over.
149 *dab*: light touch.
149 *pursed up*: drew together.
149 *crooned*: spoke in a soft, sentimental way.
149 *train*: part of a long dress that trails on the ground behind the wearer.
149 *wailed*: spoke with a complaining voice.
149 *had lost his hold*: was no longer in control of the situation.
149 *drowsing*: half asleep.
149 *withered*: dried, wrinkled with age.
149 *out of the picture*: strange; out of place.
149 *wavered*: spoke with doubt or uncertainty.
149 *little old climbing fellow*: the same 'withered ancient man', that is, Mr Neave's picture of himself.
150 *cane lounge*: comfortable chair made of cane.
151 *passion vine*: climbing plant.
151 *my treasure*: expression of affection.

154 *Looking Back*

Questions

1. When Mr Neave leaves the office, he feels a change has come over him. What is this change and what effect does it have on him?

    (a) How did Mr Neave feel when he came out of his office? (p. 145)
    (b) Had he felt like this before? (p. 145)
    (c) The Spring is described as though it were a person. What sort of person and why? (p. 145)
    (d) When Mr Neave walks home he thinks about his family. Does he think about them with pleasure? (pp. 145—146)
    (e) What adjective is repeatedly used to describe Mr Neave?

2. Why is Harold a worry to Mr Neave?

    (a) Who is Harold?
    (b) What is he like? (p. 145)
    (c) How do people react towards him and why? (pp. 145—146)
    (d) What does Harold's childhood theft show? (p. 146)
    (e) Why doesn't Mr Neave want to retire? (p. 146)

3. Visitors describe the Neaves as an 'ideal family'. Are they right? Which members of the family would agree and which wouldn't?

    (a) Where has the money come from in the Neave family, who spends most of it, and on what sort of things? (p. 146)
    (b) The reason given for the girls' not getting married is that 'They were too happy together, the girls and Charlotte.' (p. 147) Why is Mr Neave not mentioned here? What does Mr Neave think about his daughters' not marrying? Does his wife agree with him?
    (c) When Lola runs out of the music-room she nearly screams when she sees Mr Neave. Why? (p. 148)
    (d) How do the girls and his wife greet Mr Neave and what do they say to him when he arrives? (p. 148)
    (e) After they have greeted him what do they talk about and what does Mr Neave do? (pp. 148—149)

Katherine Mansfield: An Ideal Family 155

4. Half asleep, Mr Neave sees in his imagination 'a little withered ancient man climbing up endless flights of stairs'. (p. 149) What significance does this image have for the story as a whole?

   (a) Who do you think is the 'withered ancient man'? (p. 149)
   (b) What duty might start Mr Neave thinking about climbing stairs? (p. 149)
   (c) Where else in the story does Mr Neave have to climb, and how does he feel then? (p. 146)
   (d) There are many expressions in English that suggest climbing or moving upwards, such as 'climbing the ladder of success', 'building up a business', 'raising a family', etc. How do these expressions relate to Mr Neave and how does he feel about his achievements?
   (e) When Mr Neave imagines the 'ancient fellow' coming down the stairs he asks 'Why was he alone, climbing up and down?' (p. 150) How does this explain the attitude of the family towards Mr Neave?

5. Mr Neave imagines that the 'little ancient fellow' (p. 149) has turned into a spider. What is the significance of the image of the spider and its escape from the house? (p. 150)

   (a) How do people usually react to finding spiders in the house?
   (b) What positive qualities does Mr Neave have that could also be applied to spiders?
   (c) The spider slips 'past the dining room' and makes for 'the porch, the dark drive, the carriage gates, the office'. How have these places been mentioned before and how has the sequence altered? (p. 147)
   (d) Why does the spider escape from the house and go towards the office? (p. 150)
   (e) Nobody stops the spider. Why not, and why is Mr Neave horrified that nobody stops it? (p. 150)

6. When Mr Neave awakes, his thoughts go back to a farewell on a porch. Who is he saying farewell to, and what kind of leave-taking is it?

(a) Who says 'Goodbye, my treasure'? (p. 151)
(b) Is this a romantic and emotional farewell? (p. 151)
(c) Does Mr Neave remember the incident with regret? (p. 151)
(d) Is he happy with his family and wife? (p. 146)
(e) Why do you think the girl is twice described as 'little' and 'pale'? Why was she saying goodbye to Neave? What might have happened to her?

* * * * *

1. Both stories are serious stories. Which story do you feel is darker in mood?

2. Were Maria and Mr Neave happier in the past or the present? What are their chances of a happy future?

3. How far were both main characters living in the past in a world of illusions? Would it be better for Maria and Mr Neave if they still had those illusions?

4. Briefly outline the plot of each story. Is it important for a short story to have a lot of action?